COSMOS AND TRAGEDY

BROOKS OTIS

COSMOS &
TRAGEDY

AN ESSAY ON THE MEANING

OF AESCHYLUS

EDITED, WITH NOTES AND A PREFACE

BY E. CHRISTIAN KOPFF

THE UNIVERSITY OF

NORTH CAROLINA PRESS

CHAPEL HILL

© 1981 The University of North Carolina Press

Manufactured in the United States of America

Library of Congress Cataloging in Publication Data

Otis, Brooks.
   Cosmos and tragedy.

   1. Aeschylus—Criticism and interpretation.
I. Kopff, E. Christian.   II. Title.
PA3829.08   882'.01   80-25320
ISBN 0-8078-1465-2

PA
3829
.08
114,694

It was Professor Otis's desire

as conveyed by Christine Cheney Otis

that this book be dedicated

"TO MY CHILDREN"

to Brooks Adams Otis

Marion Otis Barnes

Irene Otis

Paul Hamilton Otis

and the memory of

Cheney

CONTENTS

PREFACE

Of the dead, nothing but bones," as Douglas Young used to cite a famous classical tag. It is difficult to assess the accomplishments of scholars in the humanities. Brooks Otis, when he died on July 26, 1977, had been Hobart Professor at Hobart College, where he taught from 1935 to 1957; head of the Classics Department at Stanford University from 1958 to 1970, where he became Olive H. Palmer Professor of Humanities; and Paddison Professor of Latin at the University of North Carolina at Chapel Hill from 1970 until his death. He was well known for books and articles on the major Augustan poets. He left a *Nachlass* of several completed or nearly completed books. Some colleagues knew that he had made important contributions to the study of the Greek Fathers. Much of what he tried to do may not be properly appreciated because it involved overlapping and interrelating areas of teaching and research.

Although his best-known books and articles were in literary criticism, his insights were always grounded in traditional scholarly methods. This is clearest in his approach to Ovid, where his controversial and original book *Ovid as an Epic Poet* had behind it not only stylistic analysis based on the work of Richard Heinze, but also a thorough study of Ovid's sources and Otis's Ph.D. dissertation on Ovid's manuscripts.[1] That his roots in philological method did not shut him off from development and change in understanding the meaning and significance of texts can be seen by comparing his early essay "Ovid and the Augustans"[2] with the two editions of his *Ovid*.

Different parts of the ancient world met in Otis's work, as well as different types and levels of philological method. Few contemporaries would dream of writing major essays and books on Aeschylus, Virgil, Ovid, Propertius, and the Cappadocian Fathers.

---

1. *Ovid* (Cambridge, 1966; 1970) contains a lengthy discussion of Ovid's sources in its appendix, 375–423. Otis's dissertation, "De Lactantii qui dicitur Narrationibus Ovidianis" (Harvard, 1935), was published in part in an article by the same name in *Harvard Studies in Classical Philology* 40 (1935) 209–11, and in "The Arguments of the So-called Lactantius," *Harvard Studies in Classical Philology* 41 (1936) 131–63.
2. *Transactions of the American Philological Association* 69 (1938) 188–29.

The range of his interests, his appreciation of the continuing diversity and mutual significance of Greek and Roman, pagan and Christian, reminds us of the range of the great classical scholars of the early modern era, and we know that it came directly from Otis's teaching at Hobart (as he tells us in the preface to his *Virgil: A Study in Civilized Poetry*),[3] much as the present book was inspired by a course taught at Stanford. It is typical of Otis's thought that major theological problems tended as he studied them to seek stylistic answers. His early concern with the problem of creating poetry out of a theology no longer believed, developed into his *Virgil* and *Ovid* and kept on developing to the end of his life.[4] His last work, of which the present book forms part, was an investigation of how pagan and Christian writers and thinkers attempted to "transcend tragedy," to move beyond the tragic limitations that seem built into human life. As Otis expressed it in a grant proposal, in 1972 or 1973, "Aeschylus was the first Greek author to see that a viable theodicy involved some scheme or plan for the overcoming or transcendence of tragedy."

The "originality" of Rome and the contribution of Christianity to the Greek foundations of our world were the constant themes of Otis's work, but were not often explicated at length. It is perhaps worthwhile quoting this important passage from near the end of *Virgil*:

> Aeneas thus stands for a new idea in history, the idea that *violentia* and *superbia* can be controlled, that a just *imperium* can be established, that universal peace can be a fact as well as an ideal. The Greeks were far too clever to understand this: since they could never make a durable empire, they tended to see human behaviour in either tragic or Machiavellian terms. *Humanitas* was but a theory; brutal self-seeking the hard reality; *hybris* the normal result of power; *aretē* a species of egoism. To all this kind of thinking, the Romans opposed their humanity and *pietas*, their goal of *pacis imponere morem*. (382)

And note 2 on that page:

> Here the comparison of Livy and Thucydides is very instructive. The tendency of many moderns to prefer the "realism" of Thucydides to the "moral rhetoric" of Livy begs the whole question at issue, i.e. it assumes the falsity of the

3. (Oxford, 1974) vii.
4. See "Virgilian Narrative in the Light of His Predecessors and Successors," *Studies in Philology* 73 (1976) 1–28, esp. 2, n. 1.

Roman thesis that citizens with the right character and
doctrina can literally change the course of "realistic" history.

The insights found in these few sentences not only inform most of
Otis's technical analyses of pagan and Christian literature and
philosophy, but also open up large stretches of the past to deeper
comprehension and give us tools with which to examine and
understand our own day.

Otis did not fall into the trap of reading modern ideas into
ancient works, but he never lost sight of the connections between
past and present. He did not think the Cappadocians, or Virgil, or
Aeschylus were moderns, but he knew why what they said and
did was important to us. There are hints at Christianity's answers
to the dilemmas of the ancient world and further problems raised
by those answers in his "Cappadocian Thought as a Coherent
System."[5] Unfortunately, Otis did not expatiate on these hints
either in that article or in a more popular one on Gregory Nazian-
zenus, "The Throne and the Mountain."[6] A clearer example may
be his treatment of the last scene of the *Aeneid* in *Virgil* (378–
81). Recent interpretations seem based on the authors' attitudes
towards revolt, Vietnam, and capital punishment in the world of
today, as discussion reveals and Otis was aware.[7] He was himself
convinced that Virgil approved of the death of Turnus: "The end
of the *Aeneid* is certainly not Christian. There is no reconciliation
or forgiveness in the Christian sense. Aeneas is still a man who
takes vengeance in blood . . ." (*Virgil*, 381).

Otis, I believe, assented to the inevitability, literary and moral,
of Turnus' death, as he seemed to assent to that of Cicero's. But
Otis was himself a Christian. More than that, he disapproved of
capital punishment. I remember watching the NBC news with
him in his home in Chapel Hill (he preferred NBC because John
Chancellor reminded him of one of his favorite students). A story
about capital punishment came on and he began to mutter that
capital punishment was revenge, that's all. Virgil, to Otis, was a
central figure in the development of Christian ways of thinking
and feeling, but he was not himself either a Christian or a liberal,
although Otis was both.

Many will know that his move to Stanford was the result of his
resignation from Hobart, the small college in upstate New York
where he had spent many years, teaching and thinking out his
ideas. The school fired a young man, according to Otis's thinking

5. *Dumbarton Oaks Papers* 12 (1958) 95–124.
6. *Classical Journal* 56 (1961) 146–65.
7. See "Virgilian Narrative," 27.

and others', for political reasons. A number of the faculty agreed to resign if the young man was dismissed. He was, and Otis sent in his resignation. He started to call up his friends to see how they were reacting to their new futures and new uncertainties. Otis had a reputation as an "absentminded professor." Like other academics, he sometimes cultivated the image to avoid unpleasant or wasteful duties. His years running a major graduate department and founding against all financial and administrative odds a school in Rome tell decisively against the truth of the image. In fact, the only real evidence I am aware of is his surprise and hurt when he discovered that he alone of his friends and colleagues had resigned.

His commitment to Christianity was no less real and no more obtrusive in his scholarly work than that to liberalism. There is no passage in his essays on the Fathers so self-revealing as that quoted above from *Virgil*. But one remembers his enthusiasm in barreling through the first homily in St. Basil's *Hexahemeron* in a class, or remarking à propos of Paul Tillich, "No, really, I admire the man. Spending all those years at Union Theological Seminary preaching atheism, that's really something." There is a report of his horrifying a confirmed atheist while driving from Duke to Chapel Hill by facing his passenger during a discussion, turning his eyes right away from the road, and asseverating, "Christianity without the Resurrection is SHIT."

It is more difficult to speak of his teaching. He was demanding. Years later, one could read over one's notebook and see how many exciting and compelling points had been tossed off as *obiter dicta* in lectures whose unity was easier to perceive after time and experience had brought wisdom or, at least, further thought. The most obvious monument to his commitment to teaching is the founding of the Intercollegiate Center for Classical Studies in Rome. It has introduced many young American undergraduates to the greatest symbol of the classics' living reality in today's world, the city of Rome, where Greek and Roman, Christian and pagan, still confront one another. Some of the most promising younger classicists on the American scene turned to classical studies as their permanent career because of their time at the Centro and, therefore, because of Brooks Otis.

The young American architect in Helen MacInnes's *Decision at Delphi* tells the sceptical Greek anarchist, "The past and the present aren't so far removed. They are just separate rooms in the same house, and if you unlock the doors they all connect." Brooks Otis knew that in his heart's core. He is important because in everything he did, as teacher, scholar, and administrator, he lived that feeling, that truth.

EDITORIAL NOTE

The method of the editor was modeled on that of Varius and Tucca, *ut superflua demerent, nihil adderent tamen*. All the words in the text are Professor Otis's; only the notes are mine. When in doubt I chose to keep rather than to omit. The chief omissions include (1) the original second chapter, an interesting discussion of the *Enuma Elish* and Hesiod (the latter treated along the lines of Solmsen), which was marked for omission or rewriting by Otis himself—the "Helen-episode" of the book; and (2) a last chapter, surveying in a cursory fashion Sophocles and Euripides. The present last chapter I decided to keep because of the new discussion of *Septem Contra Thebas*. On bibliography, Otis typically referred to the central works and ignored the rest, though there is good reason to think that he read them. My notes refer mainly to works mentioned in the text, but there is additional information. I should perhaps add that I believe the basic premise and "line" of the book to be correct, without subscribing to every detail and even to some major points. To have changed the style greatly would have meant rewriting, and that would have entailed the insertion of my own views. So I have omitted errors that I believe he would have caught, but have left interpretations I disagree with when I think he would have defended them. The Greek text Otis followed is eclectic and a pedantic reader will need a critical edition and an *apparatus criticus* at times. The Greekless reader will be able to follow most easily if he uses a literal translation with the Greek line numbers, such as Professor Richmond Lattimore's.

I would like to thank Mrs. Christine Otis and Professor George Kennedy as well as The University of North Carolina Press for entrusting to me the overseeing of this publication. I worked on it at the American Academy in Rome and the University of Colorado, Boulder.

COSMOS AND TRAGEDY

I. THE GUILT OF AGAMEMNON

Innumerable modern scholars and critics have attempted to define the nature of Aeschylean tragedy. It was inevitable that Aeschylus should attract them (though the literature is not so portentous as that on Dante or Shakespeare), but there is a special reason for their interest. He is peculiarly "tragic" in the starkest sense of the word and the "tragic" is a distinctly modern preoccupation. There is something unsatisfactory, indeed paradoxical, about the contemporary "picture" or "image" of Aeschylus. Modern men are interested in his tragedy, his "tragic sense of life," or his tragic art, but Aeschylus himself was interested in tragedy only so far as he could overcome or "resolve" it. The last thing he desired was tragedy for its own sake.

This paradox would not present great difficulty if it were possible to isolate Aeschylean tragedy, to understand it without its nontragic context. But Aeschylean tragedy (in the modern sense of tragedy) cannot be so isolated: it simply disappears under the attempt. The Aeschylean tragic is a product, a result, an expression of nontragic ideas and feelings. I mean something more specific than present theories of the "positive significance" of tragedy. The *Agamemnon* is not a tragedy like Sophocles' *Oedipus*, Euripides' *Hippolytus*, Shakespeare's *Macbeth*, or Ibsen's *Hedda Gabler*.

The problem emerges when we compare Aeschylus and Sophocles. They were contemporaries: all but one of Aeschylus' surviving seven plays were produced after Sophocles had won his first tragic victory in 468 B.C. Unfortunately, we lack the earlier or so-called Aeschylean plays of Sophocles. The oldest we have postdate Aeschylus' death (456) by some fourteen years. The only surviving Sophoclean play that treats the same subject as that of a surviving Aeschylean play is the *Electra*, which is late (perhaps as late as 415 B.C.).[1] Even so the difference between the two plays is more radical than a lapse of forty-three years would account for. It is even more startling than the difference between the Sophoclean and Euripidean *Electras*, striking in its way as that difference is.

The *Electra* of Sophocles is a single self-contained play, not part of a connected trilogy like Aeschylus' *Choephoroe*. One consequence

1. Albin Lesky, *Die Tragische Dichtung der Hellenen*[3] (Göttingen, 1972) 229 and n. 94.

or corollary of this is that the chief problem of Aeschylus' trilogy (the *Oresteia*) simply drops out, the problem of how to break a seemingly unbreakable chain of crimes and vengeances. There is no need to follow Orestes beyond the limits of the *Electra* since the Furies that avenge or try to avenge his crime in the *Choephoroe* and *Eumenides* have been left out. Nor was it necessary for Sophocles to preface the *Electra* by a preliminary play on the murder of Agamemnon, since that murder had lost its problematic quality. Sophocles' Agamemnon was an innocent, brutally killed by his wife and her paramour: Orestes' and Electra's vengeance was completely intelligible without any reference to the chain of crimes among which Agamemnon's murder occupied (in Aeschylus) so pivotal a place. Sophocles' Electra, in a starkly logical speech (558–609, esp. 564–576), wholly disposes of Clytemnestra's justification for her crime (vengeance for Agamemnon's sacrificial killing of Iphigenia). Agamemnon's sacrifice of Iphigenia is attributed to an accident (his unwitting killing of one of Artemis' pet stags) that entailed the immoral wrath of Artemis and her even more immoral demand for compensation through the sacrifice. Sophocles' Agamemnon has no guilt whatsover. The horror of the matricide (Orestes' murder of Clytemnestra) is played down by a deliberate concentration on Aegisthus, whose murder is made the climax of the play. That Electra (not Orestes) plays the chief role and assumes the masculine quality which Aeschylus had attributed only to Clytemnestra shifts the Aeschylean emphasis: the good boldly confronts the bad woman just as she confronts her weak and prudential sister, Chrysothemis. The play turns almost exclusively on human resolution and motive. There is a reference to Apollo as the divine sanctioner of the vengeance, but it is peripheral.

The result is modern tragedy, or the depiction of a tragic action for its own sake. Its technique, which is quite masterly, is also tragic in this sense—the conformation of the action and dialogue to the final tragic event, the murder itself at the very end of the play. The *Electra* is by no means the most tragic of Sophocles' plays, since, as Aristotle pointed out, the disaster of a bad character is not the best sort of tragedy. Here the murder itself is a righteous and triumphant vengeance and the ending can even be called "happy." But the *Antigone*, *Oedipus Rex*, and *Trachiniae* show clearly enough that Sophocles could and did construct a play to produce a sheerly tragic effect. There is no good future for the main characters of these plays. We feel at their conclusion the tragic and pitiful futility of human existence. The gods are hidden in such ambiguity that prophecy never affects or changes the event and a profound gap exists between the ignorance of the characters and the omniscience of the spectators, the famous "tragic irony" of Sophocles.

The question of human responsibility, guilt, and morality is reduced to a small compass. Aristotle pointed to this phenomenon and to the reasons for it. One cannot get a "tragic" effect from the destruction of the villain or the saint, but only from that of the good hero with some sort of flaw, a fatal readiness to blunder at the pivotal moment. A vast amount of discussion has been devoted to the flaw—the *hamartia*—and to the desiderated tragic effect, the purging (*catharsis*) of pity and fear by their dramatic presentation in the theater. This has obscured the quite limited and descriptive purpose of Aristotle's account. Assuming that one wants this sort of tragic effect, the *Oedipus Rex* is, as Aristotle insisted, the perfect model. The audience is "shocked" by the fate of a good man it can sympathize with. Because he is "good" he is not really to blame. Oedipus falls into a trap designed for him by the gods and especially by Apollo. If he had been a saint or a meticulously cautious person, he might have avoided it. He is not represented as a guilty sinner or a man with a real moral problem. The initial mistake or crime of Laius (letting Oedipus be born at all)— in other words the Aeschylean problem of inherited sin or the chain of crimes and vengeances—is taken as a datum, not a problem. The actual crimes of Oedipus (patricide and incest) are committed in ignorance and so without real moral responsibility. The justifiability of Oedipus' slaying of his father Laius (from the standpoint of Oedipus at the time of the slaying) is perhaps doubtful, but the slaying *per se* is not the cause of Oedipus' real trouble, which is his misapprehension of his paternity. That Oedipus thinks he knows, when he is actually ignorant (in this sense, blind) is a leitmotiv of the play and underlines his tragic human condition. His ignorance or blindness precludes the clear fixing of moral responsibility. The tragic effect depends upon reducing his responsibility to the smallest possible compass.

The *Oedipus Rex* is an extreme instance, but it is hard not to agree with Aristotle that it is the classic tragedy if tragedy is conceived as the deliberate excitation of pity and fear. This is what we might be if we had been in Oedipus' shoes, for are we not also ignorant of our actual condition? Is this not the very stuff of fear and sympathy? Sophocles knew that other outcomes are possible— we have the *Philoctetes* and *Oedipus Coloneus*—and none of his other heroes (Heracles or Antigone, for example) is quite like Oedipus. The moral responsibility of Heracles, Antigone, or Oedipus can never be pushed to the point of real desert or equivalence with their fates. Theodicy is, after all, not the stuff of Sophoclean tragedy.

Aeschylus stands at the opposite extreme. The main reason why the *Agamemnon* is some six hundred lines longer than each of the two other plays of the *Oresteia* trilogy, is that it includes very long choral passages concerned primarily with the guilt or moral responsibility of Agamemnon for the fate that overtakes him. His tragedy—his murder by his wife Clytemnestra—is conceived as punishment for his own misdeeds or for the nature (*ethos*) from which the misdeeds came. But Agamemnon's murder also belongs to a chain of crimes and vengeances that perpetuate each other without end. This chain is conceived as a divine necessity, the work of an ancestral spirit—*daimon*, Erinys, Moira, or Ara (curse)— whose relation to the high god, Zeus, is full of ambiguity and contradiction. The murder of Agamemnon triggers a new process by which the ambiguity is cleared up, the contradiction overcome. Everybody recognizes this fact: the last play of the trilogy—the *Eumenides*—has a "happy ending" that eliminates the possibility of similar tragedies. What is not yet clear is what the optimistic theodicy does to the actual tragedy of Agamemnon. How is the relation between moral responsibility and divine causation in Aga- memnon's case different from that of Sophocles' *Oedipus*? How does this difference affect our conception or definition of tragedy?

The first thing to do is define the real problem here. The Aes- chylean literature has dealt at length with Aeschylus' theodicy and theology or, alternatively, with his dramatic and poetical art, but not, except in a very elliptical way, with the bearing of the one on the other, the theology on the art or the art on the theology.[2] One can of course discuss the relation of Sophocles' theology and art, but the problem is not the same as in Aeschylus. Whether Sophocles is a humanist, a pessimistic atheist, or a theist who accepts both tragic and nontragic reality, he is concerned, in at least three of his plays, to get the uttermost tragic effect out of human weakness and ignorance, to stress the impossibility of human control of tragedy or, in other words, the great and truly tragic limitations of human knowledge. The excuse for calling Sophocles a humanist or pessimist—though I do not think it neces- sary to call him either—is his reluctance or even refusal to evolve a theodicy. One can hardly discuss Aeschylus without taking his theodicy into full account, but it is hard to see its dramatic and poetical significance.

2. See K. Reinhardt, *Aischylos als Regisseur und Theologe* (Bern, 1949).

Let us consider the much-disputed question of Agamemnon's guilt. In the long parodos, or first choral passage, Agamemnon is said to have been sent by Zeus Xenios (Zeus as the god of hospitality) to avenge on Troy the adultery and wife-abduction of Paris (60–62). Agamemnon and Menelaus are vultures crying for punishment against the robbers of their empty nest. But they become, in the next section of the parodos (104–20), the birds of an omen, twin eagles rending a defenseless, pregnant hare. This omen is said not only to predict the destruction of Troy but also to provoke the anger of Artemis, who resents the wanton killing of the hare and its young. Thus the hare episode is treated as much more than an omen: it is an active cause of the sacrifice of Iphigenia, the human victim that Artemis demands in requital for the hare. The sacrifice itself is said to mark a decisive change in Agamemnon's character. Faced by the terrible necessity of either abandoning his army or killing his daughter, he chooses the latter. The one entailed both disobedience of Zeus and abrogation of all his civil and military responsibilities; the other entailed a horrible inversion of his paternal feelings and responsibilities. The necessity of making such a choice is said to have hardened and coarsened his whole nature. He becomes a cruel and ruthless general, at time reckless of gods and men, the unfeeling and haughty figure who finally appears before his palace and walks the purple carpet to his death.

The whole sequence teems with difficulties. How can an omen of Troy's destruction and Agamemnon's action at Troy (as destroying eagle) cause Artemis' anger, when it is actually precedent to his going to Troy and is not literally conceived as his own act at all, but but that of the two eagles? None of the answers to this question have I think been very satisfactory.[3] Scholars have been much more successful in refuting each other than in their constructive efforts at a solution. Eduard Fraenkel has pointed out that the eagle-hare omen is a much more effective cause of Artemis' wrath than the accidental killing of the stag which Sophocles used in the *Electra* and which was originally set forth in a Cyclic epic, the *Cypria*.[4] The omen is a symbol of the destruction of Troy and gives a moral dimension to Agamemnon's guilt that the stag episode could not supply. But one can hardly stop there as Fraenkel does and consign the difficulties of the hare omen to Aeschylus' "poetical" mode of statement. His great—even dominating—concern

3. For recent thoughts on this and full bibliography to 1977, see Mark W. Edwards, "Agamemnon's Decision: Freedom and Folly in Aeschylus," *California Studies in Classical Philology* 10 (1977) 18–38.
4. *Aeschylus "Agamemnon,"* vol. 2 (Oxford, 1950) 96–99.

with Agamemnon's guilt excludes any such easy solution. Nor can we say that Agamemnon could or should have simply refused to make the sacrifice and therefore abandoned the army and the war. The war may be invested with ominous connotations, but its connection with Zeus' will, as well as its moral justification (the punishment of Paris' crime), are both made clear. Nor can one agree with H. D. F. Kitto that the human and divine motives (or motives of Artemis and Agamemnon) are distinct in such a way that the one does not determine the other.[5] The text makes this impossible: Agamemnon knows and even agonizes over the divine command. It seems evident that such writers as Albin Lesky and Jacqueline de Romilly have correctly seen that the divine and human responsibilities are inextricably connected.[6] The moral error is committed under a necessity imposed by the gods. Agamemnon changes at the moment of enforced decision, so that he takes on an internal, moral responsibility for his act and becomes a sinner who must eventually suffer for his sin. This does not mean that the objective act of sacrifice is itself converted into a sin. The text says that at this point (when confronted by the necessity) Agamemnon's nature changed and that he in consequence became something like the destroying eagle of the omen. There is ambiguity in the description of the war (first and second stasima) so that we are in doubt as to whether the war as such (or even any war as such) or only Agamemnon's conduct of the war is most reprehended. But there is little doubt that Agamemnon's conduct itself had changed. The man who returns, confronts Clytemnestra and walks the carpet is not represented as a simple innocent: he is both a successful and a harsh and prideful general. He is both responsible for and indifferent to the suffering he has caused.

Nevertheless, Agamemnon was subjected to a harsh necessity. The question whether he could have avoided the fatal change of character can only be hypothetical. What we feel is the coincidence of the necessity and the sin. So the timing of the omen (before the events it signified) and the consequent inversion of cause and effect, as well as the ambiguity of the omen itself, are disturbing only on the most narrowly logical interpretation. Agamemnon was envisaged as a man whose whole career was determined, so that the time sequence made little difference. The omen

5. *Form and Meaning in Drama* (London, 1956) 1–8.

6. See Lesky's "Decision and Responsibility in the Tragedy of Aeschylus," *Journal of Hellenic Studies* 86 (1966) 78–85, and de Romilly's "Vengeance humaine et vengeance divine: remarques sur l'*Orestes* d'Eschyle," *Das Altertum*, Festschrift W. Schadewaldt (Stuttgart, 1970) 65–77.

rightly depicted how he would change and act: his sacrifice of Iphigenia and his harshness as a general at Troy are part of the same character. The fact of decision, of change, of sin, is the important thing, not its date or logically sequential position.

Agamemnon is caught up by a necessity that he did not create and in fact abhorred. The initial necessity which changed his character was imposed from without by the gods. He could be punished for being the kind of man who would change under such a necessity—he is represented as responsible for the change—but he certainly did not enjoy, much less initiate, the necessity himself. We can perhaps say that Artemis anticipated his action at Troy and proleptically punished him for it, because she already recognized in him an *ethos* which would change under pressure. But we cannot avoid the *external* pressure of the necessity. He is not represented as simply bad or sinful. His sin is in part involuntary. Thyestes and Atreus were sinners in a different sense, as were later Clytemnestra and Aegisthus, though these two were also involved in some sort of necessity. Each had a crime to avenge and each was driven by a supernatural power, the *daimon* or Erinys of the house. But the distinction between them and Agamemnon is clear: the guilt of Agamemnon is far less deliberate, far less absolute. He is also a great general and king who did not in the least deserve his terrible and disgraceful death. The very ambiguity of his conduct poses a new question. What was the justification of the necessity and how could it be overcome? In what way could the justice of Zeus be realized? The very doubtfulness of Agamemnon's guilt marked the beginning of a new question, a new stage or kind of justice.

From this standpoint the tragedy of Agamemnon, compared to Atreus, Thyestes, Aegisthus, or Clytemnestra, is almost Sophoclean or Aristotelian. He is a good man with a *hamartia*, or moral flaw, brought out by a divinely imposed necessity, a fatal trap or dilemma that he could not foresee or avoid. But Aeschylus is very un-Sophoclean in his treatment of Agamemnon's murder. Instead of terminating a self-contained tragedy concerned with the awful futility and blindness of human existence, he raises the demand for more justice and enlightenment. The play breaks the ambiguity and ignorance of the past and forces a decision, a new relationship of gods and men. The murder is a great cosmic event as well as a decisive event in the house of Atreus and the history of the *polis*.

The true importance of Agamemnon's guilt is defined by its ambiguity. The guilt is too great to be exorcised by anything short of his death. The guilt of Clytemnestra is much greater and not at

all ambiguous. By the next play, the *Choephoroe*, the balance between guilt and innocence is changed. Orestes is no Agamemnon,
but a man whose guilt is only a minor accompaniment of the
divine necessity by which he is bound. The problem changes from
one of guilt to one of necessity itself and of the divine orders
behind it. The murder of Clytemnestra finally raises the level of
dramatic action from the human to the divine sphere with which
the last play, the *Eumenides*, deals.

The ambiguous nature of the connection between divine necessity and human responsibility is crucial. In Sophocles this is taken
for granted. His sort of tragedy depends on the fact that no one
can be called happy until his life is completed, or removed from
the ambiguity—the ignorance—which up to the very last moment
conceals the possibility of a most frightful reversal of his prior life-
pattern. Sophoclean tragedy maintains and magnifies this ambiguity, regards it as an unalterable, inevitable part of the human
condition. This is why human life is so "tragic." Aeschylus stresses
the ambiguity because it cannot be permanent; it must be cleared
up. He is concerned not with one human condition but with
two—with the old, Sophoclean ignorance or confusion of divine
and human wills and with a new, Aeschylean enlightenment in
which the relation of the divine and human is clarified and made
intelligible.

Aeschylean scholars have fallen into considerable confusion
here. Lesky, for example, has stressed the conjunction of divine
and human causes. The gods cause an action for which men are
made responsible. "To conclude our observations," he says, "we
may take it as proved that two elements of high significance in
Aeschylus can be clearly shown: the close union of necessity imposed by the gods and the personal decision to act. This union
leaves a certain space for the will of the individual but at the
same time limits it."[7] He fails, however, to discriminate between
instances of the "union." He writes as if the same thing held
for Xerxes, Eteocles, Pelasgos, Agamemnon, Clytemnestra, and
Orestes. He even seems to feel that Aeschylus deliberately left the
nature of the union in obscurity and quotes with apparent ap-
proval the remark of Virginia Woolf that "there is [in Aeschylus]
an ambiguity which is the mark of the highest poetry." I am afraid
that he has laid himself open to the sort of interpretation we find
in Hugh Lloyd-Jones's article "The Guilt of Agamemnon."[8] To

7. "Decision and Responsibility," 85.
8. *Classical Quarterly* 12 (1962) 187–99; see also *The Justice of Zeus* (Berkeley
and Los Angeles, 1971) and his translation of the *Oresteia* (Englewood
Cliffs, 1970).

Lloyd-Jones, Agamemnon is, like the characters of the *Iliad*, deceived or deliberately blinded by an *ate* set on him by the Erinys and by Zeus himself. The whole thing is primitive and amoral and there is no real justice at all. "From his birth Agamemnon's fate," says Lloyd-Jones, "like that of Oedipus or Eteocles, has been determined; he is the son of the accursed Atreus. Zeus uses him as the instrument of his vengeance upon Troy; but he uses him in such a fashion that his own destruction must inevitably follow."[9]

Lesky does not follow Lloyd-Jones's somewhat simplistic view of Aeschylus' theology, but he does not provide us with a real alternative. So long as we do not discriminate between notions of guilt, there cannot be an alternative, for Aeschylus recognized that a primitive situation—a substantial absence of justice—had existed and still existed at the beginning of the *Agamemnon*. Aeschylus, so far from being happy with the ambiguity of Agamemnon's guilt or with the absence of a clear-cut divine justice in his case, is concerned to show the intolerable situation which resulted. His hope is that Zeus will resolve it, and this happens.

The *drama* of Aeschylus is precisely designed to resolve the ambiguity that Lesky and Lloyd-Jones seem to regard as exhibited and perpetuated by it. We can thus explain the nature of the drama itself—on both its technical and its moral sides. All see the "Hesiodic" theology, the conflict of old and new gods and their final reconciliation. All or at least the great majority acknowledge the author's concern with human guilt and responsibility. But the relation of the two has remained obscure. If they reject a primitive view of Aeschylus' theology like that of Lloyd-Jones, critics are unable to explain the indubitably primitive elements in the *Agamemnon*. If they base their interpretations on these primitive elements, they cannot explain the transformation of these elements in the ensuing drama. Nor are they troubled by the curious fact that, on their theory, Aeschylus was confined to a thought-world some centuries prior to his own time. The result is considerable confusion which has obscured the dramatic structure or movement of the trilogy. It is essential to be clear about the "ambiguity" of Aeschylus, if we are to understand him as either a dramatist or a theologian. This book is accordingly an exercise in clarification.

9. "Guilt of Agamemnon," 199.

Most modern readers of the *Oresteia* are much more impressed by the *Agememnon* than by the other two plays. What stands out is the murder of Agamemnon, not the murder of Clytemnestra or the court scene of the *Eumenides*. Indeed, the rest of the trilogy appears to be an appendage. Once he is killed, he must be avenged, and once he is avenged, his vengeance must be made to stick and not be defeated by the counter-vengeance of his wife's representatives, the Furies. In another sense the *Agamemnon* seems isolated from the rest of the trilogy. In that play we are concerned above all with the guilt of Agamemnon as it bears on the Trojan War, the sacrifice of Iphigenia, and the sins of the house of Atreus. Thereafter the question of Agamemnon's guilt disappears; the emphasis is on Clytemnestra's guilt and even more on the guilt or innocence of Orestes. There is a brief allusion to the entire sequence of events in the house of Atreus at the very end of the *Choephoroe* (1065–76), but in the *Eumenides* the problem is Orestes' guilt (vis-à-vis Clytemnestra's), and the house of Atreus is not mentioned. Agamemnon's death marks the decisive turning point, the point that separates past from present and future and enables a solution of the problem of guilt. This is why his tragedy—or murder—looms so large and why it seems to sum up and at the same time push aside the problems of the house of Atreus, the problems that dominate the *Agamemnon* itself.

From such considerations we might reach the apparently paradoxical conclusion that the guilt of Agamemnon is both stressed and discounted, or that the *Choephoroe* contradicts the *Agamemnon* and changes the emphasis of the trilogy. Agamemnon's tragedy is the event that shifts and eventually removes altogether the burden of guilt from the house of Atreus and from all houses or people similarly subjected to an apparently self-perpetuating chain of guilt and crime. The drama of Agamemnon's murder telescopes the past and brings it into the open where it can be defined and dealt with. As a result, Orestes' guilt assumes a totally different character, as do the actions of Apollo (Zeus) on the one hand and of the non-Olympian powers on the other. The tragedy of Agamemnon is the principal sacrifice that brings peace both cosmic and political, or the human event that sets in motion the contest of the supernatural powers and the "new Creation" that the victory of the good powers makes possible. In one sense the guilt of Agamemnon is expiated by his death; in another sense he is the good man murdered by the evil woman in such a way that the whole character and meaning of guilt and vengeance are changed. We move from past ambiguity into present and future clarity.

The importance of viewing the *Oresteia* in this way is that it greatly facilitates our understanding of its *dramatic* character. We can see *why* Aeschylus arranges the episodes and choruses as he does and why the poetry is fused with the action as it is. To a certain extent, scholars, particularly Bruno Snell and Jacqueline de Romilly,[1] have correctly described this peculiarly Aeschylean sort of tragedy—its emphasis on active decision, its dilation or thickening of the tragic moment and enormous buildup of tension around it, its excitation of *phobos*, dreadful expectation, as opposed to the Euripidean concern with *pathos* and the pathetic—but they have not, I think, really explained its essential raison d'être, which we can best define as the tragic resolution of a dreadful ambiguity. Aeschylus wanted to portray a tragic event which would permit the right kind of resolution. The vengeance of Atreus on Thyestes was that of one criminal on another, of a frightful murderer on a shameless adulterer. So long as such crimes succeeded one another there could be no hope of breaking the chain of guilt and vengeance. In each case the sinner deserved his fate. A vengeance was needed that would be out of all proportion to the crime avenged and would thus set the avenger in opposition to *dike*, or justice. So a final vengeance on the evil avenger would approximate *dike* and require the support of the god (Zeus) who already stood for *dike*. Guilt had to be reduced to such a point that further vengeance would mock the very name of justice. Only in such a situation would Zeus be called upon to uphold his theodicy, and the rule of *dike* be clearly opposed to the older rule of mere retaliation. Aeschylus had to change the balance of guilt but not to eliminate guilt altogether. All retribution was for guilt of some sort: the problem was not to abandon retribution but to make it just or consistent with a genuine theodicy.

Agamemnon approximates the flawed hero of Aristotle's *Poetics*. But his fate is not merely tragic—in Aristotle's and Sophocles' sense—but genuinely sacrificial, or, more exactly, a curious and dreadful blend of punishment and sacrifice. This is why it is so

1. See Snell, *Aischylos und das Handeln im Drama*, *Philologus* Supplement-band 20, 1 (Leipzig, 1929); *The Discovery of the Mind* (Cambridge, Mass., 1953); *Scenes from Greek Tragedy* (Berkeley and Los Angeles, 1964); and de Romilly, *Time in Greek Tragedy* (Ithaca, 1968).

shocking and so problematic, why it sets in motion so much more than the retributive powers that had heretofore been at work.

Aeschylus had to show (1) that Agamemnon's guilt was part and parcel of the guilt of his house, of the past, and was bound to incur the retribution that ran in his house; (2) that the retribution was also excessive and wicked; and (3) that this very fact had cosmic significance. He had (1) to emphasize both the guilt and the greatness (or eminent virtue) of Agamemnon, both the punishment incurred by the first and the obligation of vengeance demanded by the second; (2) to build up the evil eminence of Clytemnestra, the great excess of guilt over justification in her crime; and (3) to bring out the extrahuman or divine forces at work in both characters. He was concerned not with the tragic fate of man in general but with the cosmic question posed by the fate of a particular sort of man, a particular dramatic moment. If it were posed with enough salience, it would almost inevitably receive an answer. The ambiguity in which human and divine existence had heretofore been veiled would burst open in spectacular horror, with sufficiently explosive force to change the cosmic and political orders, to create a new world.

The task for his tragic art was one of expanding or dilating a single tragic act or moment into a panorama of human and divine life—the entire past of the house of Atreus and the Trojan War; the enigmatic designs of Zeus and the dark Erinyes. The moment was the return and immediately ensuing murder of Agamemnon. This, though really one moment since Agamemnon is killed almost as soon as he returns, is for dramatic purposes divided into a series of episodes each of which comes at a (dramatically) shorter interval from the other and from the murder itself: the sighting of the beacon; the celebration of its good news; the herald; the entrance of Agamemnon and Cassandra; the interval between Agamemnon's and Cassandra's exits into the palace.

Between these events, each of which progressively increases tension and fearful expectation, come the choral passages and finally the kommos and dialogue of Cassandra and chorus. Here the event is set in a frame of human interpretation (the chorus) that clearly anticipates the crime to come. Though the chorus is ostensibly celebrating Agamemnon's victory over Troy, it does so in such a way that victory is turned into woe. Its emphatic silence about and ambiguous hints at the true situation in Argos are reinforced by the ambiguity of its lyrics—their ambiguous mixture of apparent joy and actual woe. The chorus knows that events have taken place and are about to take place that challenge both the justice of Zeus and the morality of man. Against this human ambiguity and doubt is set a divine voice, that of the prophetess Cassandra, which breaks through the veil of poetry into "prosaic" utterance (in iambic trimeter), but not so as to affect or change the foreordained tragedy. The aged chorus had dealt with Troy and Agamemnon's role there and with the war-guilt that came of his slaying of Iphigenia; Cassandra, Trojan though she was, deals with the quite different scene at Argos, the woes endemic in the house of Atreus. It is remarkable how the two complementary voices—the human one of the chorus, the divinely inspired one of Cassandra—expand the scope and meaning of the tragic moment of Agamemnon's death. There is first a combination of retrospect and foreboding; then, finally, with Cassandra, a more explicit combination of retrospect and prophecy, in which past and future are made to swell the actual time of drama. But this is not all: both the chorus and Cassandra see all this in a supernatural light that grows from vague conjectures about the divine to the actual divine presence in Cassandra. The divinity is at hand and strikes!

This lyrical development is inserted into the action: the stasima and kommoi are unintelligible without the episodes. While the parados and stasima concentrate on the war, and the guilt of Agamemnon as connected with it, and are ominously silent—with the sort of silence that speaks—about the guilt of Clytemnestra, she herself is the true center of the drama; her hypocritical inversion of the truth, her masculine energy, dominate the episodes. The living Agamemnon is the center of only one brief scene, and this too is dominated by Clytemnestra, who makes him walk the carpet to his doom. All this time the guilt of Clytemnestra has been silently building up. Its eruption in the Cassandra kommos and in her brutal revelation of the corpses requires the final full confrontation of chorus and Clytemnestra. As last the guilt problem is seen in a different light: it is no longer Agamemnon's but Clytemnestra's guilt that is at issue; it is no longer the will of Zeus but the dreadful Erinyes of the house of Atreus, that raises the great theological question, the question of *dike*. With Aegisthus' belated appearance at the end, the whole locus of guilt has shifted and the next, Oresteian, phase of the problem has begun.

We must constantly bear in mind that all this is poetry with different functions, but poetry nonetheless. The various aspects of this poetry—the different rhythms and metaphors, sound-sense correspondences, narrative passages, moral reflections, recurring symbols or leitmotivs—all express and reflect the drama going on; it is intrinsically different from the nondramatic lyric of Pindar or the narrative of Homer. For the guilts of Agamemnon or Clytemnestra are not related in a narrative or exemplary way but shown at work. This is true of any poetical drama, but in Aeschylus the drama is invested with a momentum and duration which we might call "trans-tragic," something designed to outrun and overtop any possible denouement. The tragedy is cosmic transformation: the central event—the murder of Agamemnon—is designed to reach out and change all the previous expectations of men. To say that the poetry has a special dramatic vitality means little unless we see concretely how the dramatic and poetic elements (to distinguish for purposes of analysis what are really inseparable) support one another in this particular drama. The various elements of the poetical drama—the iambic trimeter episodes, the parodos, the stasima, the kommoi, and the epirremata—have each a special dramatic function, a function connected with the actions and viewpoints of the *dramatis personae*.

It is not simply the voice of Aeschylus or the superpersonal mind of the author but that of specific people, the puzzled yet reflective and in a sense theologically concerned elders of Argos, men who have lived through a long experience with the house of Atreus, who have seen the war start and continue for ten long years while at home they have witnessed or heard about unmentionable doings in the palace. They are groping for understanding, for a clue to the designs of Zeus, not because they are disinterested philosophers but because they have a stake in Argos, because they hope, despite all counterevidence, for the best outcome. But their puzzlement, their theological perturbation, cannot be taken at face value. That they speak in lyrical measures, in the language of poetry, is not simply due to the convention which decrees such measures and language for choral parodoi and stasima. The distinction between their lyrics and the action (the iambic trimeter episodes) is due also to their inactive status. They are useless old men, dream shadows as they call themselves (82), who can only look on and reflect—whom the call to action throws into the uttermost confusion and bewilderment. To take their reflections on necessity and the gods as so many keys to the whole drama is to lose sight of their human identity. They have no assured access to the divine mystery of the will of Zeus. Their concern with the war, with Helen, with the war-guilt of both the Trojans and the Atridae, reflects their status as the elders of Argos and brings out the political bearing of the domestic events: the adultery of Helen, and Menelaus' and Agamemnon's confusion of personal with public motives. The lyrical distance of the chorus corresponds to its dramatic role.

The episodes that are dominated by Clytemnestra (except when she is arranging and preparing the murder inside the palace) are necessarily unreflective, and calculated to conceal rather than reveal the meaning of events, to represent the expected and realized return of Agamemnon as a wonderful triumph and escape from danger, the homecoming of a perfect hero. The truth is brought out by the frustrated prophetess, Cassandra, and finally by the actual revelation of the murder when the "unmasked" Clytemnestra confronts the chorus with the brutal facts. Clytemnestra in her hypocrisy and her terrible frankness calls the tune throughout.

We thus get in the final kommoi and epirrhemata a mixture of action (or speech in iambic trimeter) and lyric reflection (in lyric meters) which reflects at last the involvement of the chorus in the action as it successively confronts Cassandra and the new truth-speaking Clytemnestra. What the chorus says on its own, in the parodos and stasima, is different from what it hears from Cassandra and from what it says when forced by Clytemnestra to face the naked truth. To take all the choral pronouncements as being extradramatic on a special, high level of truth is to miss their dramatic force and meaning. In particular the doctrine of an indissoluble union between divine necessity and human responsibility set forth in the parodos is contradicted by the final kommos. The truth emerges from the action; the chorus is anything but a prophet or an assured moralist. The ambiguity of its poetry expresses the ambiguity of its dramatic self or persona.

To reduce such a dense poetical-dramatic structure to an analytical scheme is impossible. We can make some observations that will illustrate the general propositions just set forth.

(1) The prologue (1–39) starts the special time sequence of the play and indeed of the whole trilogy. The special Aeschylean moment has begun with a flash of light in the night and a high shriek (ἰοὺ ἰού, 25; ὀλολυγμὸν, 28). Key and tone are set; so also is their double significance. The watchman knows that all is far from well, that the walls of Atreus' house could tell a tale. He is at once a humble peasant and a sort of cosmic observer. The ambiguous domestic references, the obvious double entendres (such as the injunction to Clytemnestra to leap from her bed to greet the beacon, 27), and the mixed notes of joy and woe—especially evident in the juxtaposition of the beacon that turns night into day (and will set the chorus dancing in the city) with the evil plight (συμφορὰν, 18) of the house, or in the coupling of the fear that dispels sleep with the joy that overcomes it, in the blend of happiness and dread at the master's expected return—are from the start set against a cosmic frame: that of the starry heaven and the night. The fire signal itself gives cosmic significance to the moment (Troy's fall

and Agamemnon's ensuing return). The contrast of the victor in the far distance and the "expectant male-willed" woman in the palace below (γυναικὸς ἀνδρόβουλον ἐλπίζον κέαρ, 11) anticipates a great deal of the opening drama. The dominant note of this extraordinarily dense passage is the blending of weal and woe, the sense of tragic ambiguity. The lines νῦν δ' εὐτυχὴς γένοιτ' ἀπαλλαγὴ πόνων / εὐαγγέλου φανέντος ὀρφναίου πυρός (20–21) are typical of the whole passage: the cries of woe and joy, the past and the present (τὰ πρόσθ', 19; νῦν, 20), the light and the dark (νυκτὸς ἡμερήσιον φάος, 22–23), happiness and toils, and the expectation of change (ἀπαλλαγὴ πόνων, 20) followed by the dramatic coming of change (ὦ χαῖρε λαμπτήρ, νυκτὸς ἡμερήσιον / φάος, 22).

The watchman is the first of a series of characters (the herald, Agamemnon himself, Cassandra, Aegisthus) who appear in only one episode. Aside from the chorus, Clytemnestra alone appears in several episodes (in all but the prologue and the Cassandra scene). It is her action, her guilt, that determines the basic change of the trilogy. But we must see the situation from several points of view. The chorus and Cassandra are the most significant, but even the watchman and the herald have their own points of view, their own dramatically appointed roles. The watchman is the ordinary man of Argos, whose interest in his own physical hardships is characteristic. That such a man—who is necessarily excluded from the society of the palace to which both the chorus and the herald have access—should see the double significance, the weal and woe, of the victory and return of Agamemnon, tells us something that the chorus could not, and anticipates and enhances the message of the chorus. The watchman, unlike the chorus, has the domestic Argive point of view; he has seen what has been going on at the palace, and his enigmatic references set the tone of the first two-thirds of the drama: the sense of a great evil that cannot be proclaimed or overtly uttered but which yet underlies the whole action. The ambiguities of the chorus, the hypocrisy of Clytemnestra, the honest puzzlement of the herald, the insensitivity of Agamemnon, all, in their different ways, confirm this. Only Cassandra speaks out, but she is doomed to be misunderstood.

All this comes out in the very language of the watchman's speech. His metaphors and turns of phrase are aspects of the whole play—for they introduce leitmotivs that constantly recur—and characteristic of his own lower-class personality. His references to the fall of dice, the great ox that silences his tongue, his dog-like position on the housetop, his dread of going to sleep, are in one sense quite as natural or peasant-like as his simple acceptance of nature—night, stars, the succession of seasons, the cold dew, light and sound—but, in another, they prefigure the inversion of nature in the house of Atreus, and particularly in Clytemnestra, by whom they are all hypocritically transformed.

(2)(a) The long parodos (40–257, or 218 lines) has as its dramatic excuse the desire of the Argive elders to learn from Clytemnestra what good news has induced her to offer sacrifices all over the city. This is what brought them to the palace (85–91, 258–63). Yet the choral passage does not reflect or anticipate the beacon fire. It takes up the ambiguity and expectancy of that part of the watchman's speech which preceded the sighting of the beacon (1–21). Its predominant note is again the ambiguous union of weal and woe: αἴλινον αἴλινον εἰπέ, τὸ δ' εὖ νικάτω (159). Their appearance is determined by the excitement of seeing the beacon. Troy is in all men's minds. Their words show the grim expectancy, the tension of war: δέκατον μὲν ἔτος τόδ' ἐπεὶ Πριάμῳ (40). This moment (τόδ', 40) marks the passage of ten years and the coming of a future which is at once anticipated weal and anticipated woe. The emphasis on the ambiguity of life (its weal and woe) that marks the parodos is connected with the dramatic present of the war's end and the hopes and forebodings that go with it. The whole Trojan War—above all Agamemnon's part in it—is an inextricable blend of good and bad which is directly related to the situation in Argos, the situation to which, it is hoped and feared, Agamemnon will return. This domestic aspect of the ambiguity is only touched on in the parodos and the three stasima that follow. They and the intervening episodes all ostensibly deal with Troy, with the great victory there, and the misfortune of the Greeks who do or do not return. The domestic scene is the subject of deliberately enigmatic reference that shows awareness of the gross hypocrisy of Clytemnestra but never goes beyond the darkest of hints. The obvious disparity between the somber tone and the happy occasion (victory and return) of the choral lyrics echoes the similar disparity of the watchman's words. Only an outsider (i.e., Cassandra) can come out with the domestic truth. But there is more to it than this: the chorus is genuinely puzzled—it is man before a superhuman enigma—and cannot reveal the truth known only to gods. The whole truth can only come out of the drama itself. Cassandra's words will be enigmatic; they can have no direct bearing upon the event. Yet the cumulative effect of the choral stasima and the Cassandra kommos is to set the event in its proper context, to magnify it to the point where it becomes equal to the immense revolution it is designed to produce.

The parodos, the three following stasima, and the intervening episodes (before the murder) reveal the same ambiguity in the guilts of Agamemnon and Clytemnestra. Clytemnestra's blatant hypocrisy is designed to excite in the spectator the revulsion that will reach its climax with the murder itself. We need to know not so much her motive for the murder (this is never thought of as justifiable) but Agamemnon's own involvement in the guilt of his house and his own moral responsibility. What was the meaning of his sacrifice of domestic to public concerns, the bearing of his Trojan on his Argive or Greek motives? The question is never one of his salvation—he is doomed from the start—but of the results that flow from the very ambiguity of his guilt. If he had been simply innocent, all the talk about Zeus' *dike*—about the morality of power—would have been futile and the problem of human and divine justice would never have emerged. If he had been as guilty as Clytemnestra, there would have been no point to the drama, no need for the vengeance of Orestes. Agamemnon paid a terrible price for his victory at Troy—both what he did to Iphigenia and the penalty that followed—and it is this that we must understand if his murder is to be more than an isolated event and not an essential link between past and future.

The parodos and the first three stasima invest Agamemnon with an almost unbearable weight of historical and cosmic meaning. The human past and the morality of Zeus and the gods are centered on him. Otherwise his fate could hardly have been a cosmic fact, a means of bringing in a new divine and human dispensation. The action of his return and murder would by itself have been quite unequal to so portentous a significance. If we had not been shown that Agamemnon carried on his shoulders the responsibility or "guilt" of the war, a responsibility inextricably bound up with his domestic responsibility (as the sacrificer of Iphigenia), and that the gods, including Zeus, were heavily involved in his actions, we could not have taken him as an exemplary figure standing for the whole past or old dispensation. He is, however, representative of the good and evil of the old dispensation and the righteousness that is also contained in it. He is the Zeus-sent avenger of Paris' crime and the crime of the Trojans; he is also the man who preferred the life of the bad Helen to that of the good Iphigenia and underwent a frightful change of character in consequence. He is exemplary and his murder is a sort of vicarious sacrifice. He is neither simply bad nor simply good but involved in a whole regime of guilt for which he is only partly responsible. For the regime itself is at fault and it is this that has to be shown, if his fate is to be taken as a truly cosmic event.

This exemplary magnification of Agamemnon is dramatically

conceived. The choruses are directly related to the action. They reveal a dramatic movement that merges past with present and future, distant cause with present effect and with fear of what impends. Unlike the choruses of Pindar or Stesichorus, they are progressive, made up of metrically different triads or pairs of strophes, and never return upon their beginnings in the sort of "ring composition" so typical of nondramatic lyric. An analysis of the parodos will show this.

The anapaestic introduction (40–103) is both a marching piece— marking the actual entrance of the chorus—and a link between the trimeters and the lyrics to follow. The first thirty-two lines (40–71) fix the date and describe the departure of the Atridae for Troy—it is the tenth year since then. The Atridae are compared to vultures circling a deserted nest (the "nest" of Menelaus). A god—Apollo, Pan, or Zeus—hears their shrill cries and sends the symbolic vultures against Paris of Troy. They are the Erinyes of sinners, though they are avengers sent by Zeus himself, Zeus Xenios, the god who is bound to strike down a man who has violated the laws of hospitality. The result is the terrible war, all for a promiscuous woman. This is how it now is; the outcome will be as destined. No amount of sacrifices or libations can change it.

Then the chorus in the remaining thirty-two lines (the second half of the anapaestic section) turns to its own personal situation. They are useless dream shapes that haunt the day, because of their age unfit for the war at Troy, yet eager to hear news from Clytemnestra. What has caused her to make all these sacrifices? The whole city is alight with them. Perhaps she can heal their anxiety— perhaps even dispel their concern by hope. At the outset we see the ambiguity of the war, of its cause (the reft nest versus the promiscuous woman), of the sacrifices, of anything that can help or hinder destiny. The pivotal light and sound motifs (βωμοὶ δώροισι φλέγονται· / ἄλλη δ᾽ ἄλλοθεν οὐρανομήκης λαμπὰς ἀνίσχει, 91– 92; κλάζοντες, 48; γόον ὀξυβόαν, 57) are repeated, and they indicate the ambivalence of the chorus' mind: who knows whether they signify weal or woe, divine help or immutable fate?

(b) The chorus then moves into an animated triad of dactylic stanzas (strophe, antistrophe, and epode). The increase of emotion and lyrical intensity is marked:

> κύριός εἰμι θροεῖν ὅδιον κράτος αἴσιον ἀνδρῶν
> ἐντελέων· ἔτι γὰρ θεόθεν καταπνεύει
> πειθώ, μολπᾶν ἀλκάν, σύμφυτος αἰών·   (104–6)

We are back at the start of the expedition, but at a slightly later stage, marked by a later and different omen: it is no longer Zeus himself who sends it but his terrible representatives, the warlike eagles that rend the pregnant hare hard by the royal palace of the Atridae. The omen is one of disturbing ambiguity ("sing woe, woe but may the good win out!" is the last verse of each of the three strophes), as Calchas, the seer, recognizes. It predicts the Atridae's conquest of Troy but it also arouses the enmity of Artemis, who from her love of all young animals hates the "eagles' banquet," their destruction of the hare's unborn progeny, and is preparing the terrible calm that will hold up the expedition, require the sacrifice of Iphigenia, and evoke the unforgetting, child-avenging Wrath which will follow. The forlorn vultures and *their* vengeance on their enemies have been replaced by the triumphant eagles and Artemis' vengeance on them. The reversal of the first image by the second is striking. In the first, the birds are bereft or righteously grieved; in the second, they are themselves the bereavers, the unrighteously triumphant. Divine power both aids and punishes: the deed of the avengers is avenged; Troy is both justly and impiously destroyed. We feel the ambiguity of the guilt, its fluctuation from one side to the other (first Trojan, then Greek, first of Paris, then of the Atridae), and also its ambiguous and fluctuating relation to the gods (Zeus, Artemis). This fluctuation is to mark all the ensuing stasima (especially the first two). But the special emphasis here is on the guilt of the Atridae. The emotional dactyls that start the strictly lyric part of the parodos set forth the basis of the chorus's forebodings: the expected victory is somehow tainted at its source.

(c) The pace then slows to two pairs of slightly but significantly different trochaic strophes. The change of pace and accent (rising rather than falling as in the dactyls) shifts the mood to one of reflective prayer. The events of the preceding dactylic strophes seem to be broken off. But this is only a poetical-dramatic device that accentuates the next of the fearful chain of events:

> Ζεύς, ὅστις ποτ' ἐστίν, εἰ τόδ' αὐ-
> τῷ φίλον κεκλημένῳ,
> τοῦτό νιν προσεννέπω.   (160–62)

Because Zeus is the only present god (he has shown his victorious power by vanquishing Ouranos and Kronos), he can successfully impose the law of learning by suffering (τὸν πάθει μάθος / θέντα κυρίως ἔχειν, 177–78). It is the χάρις βίαιος (182), or blessing, that the Olympian gods from their dread seats of power so forcefully assert. Even the unwilling will learn wisdom or restraint (σωφρονεῖν, 181). This Agamemnon (καὶ τόθ' ἡγεμών, 184) learned at Aulis when he refused to blame Calchas for his ominous prophecy. The

so-called Zeus-prayer is not after all an interruption of the movement of the parodos[2] but an essential part of it. Agamemnon at this
particular crisis—the omen as interpreted by Calchas—illustrated
the principle *pathei mathos*, of learning by suffering.

Those who call this prayer the moral or key of the trilogy have
not paid enough attention to its placement and its deliberate ambiguity. Zeus, the chorus seems to be saying, has in all his plenitude
of new power—in virtue of his victory over the old gods, a victory
that the chorus accepts—laid down a new law and grace, a law
that brings wisdom by suffering even against men's will, a grace
that is violently enforced. Agamemnon does not seek to avoid the
terrible dilemma in which he is put by Calchas' revelation of the
divine will. He does not blame him for his words; he "breathes
with" the blasts of fortune or accepts the evil that they bring.

In what respect is Agamemnon's dilemma a lesson in wisdom?
What does he learn by his suffering or his abasement before Zeus'
will? These questions are not answered, certainly not here. The
trochees express the chorus's demand for a visible theodicy. The
solemnity of these two trochaic pairs of strophes—the deliberate
change of pace and mood that they introduce—fixes our attention
on the meaning of the event they describe. The problem of Zeus'
justice centers on it. Suffering teaches wisdom—that seems to be
not only the chorus's but Aeschylus' conviction—but how Zeus'
blow will bring it about is left utterly obscure. Agamemnon's
preliminary compliance with the lesson of Zeus—his pious acceptance of Calchas' prophecy—is but one stage of his reaction to it.
The second stage is very different.

(d) The shift from dactyls (104–59) to trochees (160–92) was
dramatic, but it was dramatic in the sense of a calm before a storm
or a moment of reflection before the climax of a tragedy. With the
iambs of the next two strophes (193–217) the wisdom of Agamemnon becomes violently agitated and we see his decision in
dramatic, not reflective terms. The meter not only shifts from
trochaic to iambic measure but shifts to a special, peculiarly ominous and "tragic" sort of iamb. The first two lines are of the
pattern πνοαὶ δ' ἀπὸ Στρυμόνος μολοῦσαι / κακόσχολοι, νήστιδες,
δύσορμοι (193–194). These are usually called "syncopated iambs,"
a label that tells us little. The important thing is the interruption
and shift of the iambic rhythm after the first two iambic feet: in
effect the iambs become trochees or a trochaic replaces an iambic

2. See R. D. Dawe, "The Place of the Hymn to Zeus in Aeschylus'
Agamemnon," *Eranos* 64 (1966) 1–21; and Albin Lesky, *Die Tragische Dichtung
der Hellenen*[3] (Göttingen, 1972) 116 and n. 69.

pattern; or we can even descry dochmiac (ἀπὸ Στρυμόνος) developing out of the iambs into the cretic. What is essential, however, is to see the actual rhythm, not the metrical explanation. The iambs are in any event interrupted: the initial iambic rhythm is altered or distorted with a resulting feeling of difficulty, contradiction or strain.

George Thompson is perhaps a little fanciful when he says of these lines, "Does not this straining effect, this tense struggle between dochmiac and trochaic, suggest as clearly as rhythm can the straining of the ropes as the fleet lies at anchor, pitching and rolling in the storm?"[3] But he *has* seen the "strain," though I would locate it more particularly in the shift of meter after the fourth syllable. Both the strain of the contrary winds and the strain of Agamemnon's dilemma are brought out in the corresponding verse of the antistrophe, βαρεῖα μὲν κὴρ τὸ μὴ πιθέσθαι (206), where the shift or interruption comes on βαρεῖα μὲν κὴρ, the dreadful fate itself. The rest of each strophe shows the same sort of strain—e.g., from 195 to 196 and in 198, until in 199 it breaks into choriambs (the penultimate six of which are continuous):

> προφέρων Ἄρτεμιν, ὥστε χθόνα βάκτροις
> ἐπικρούσαντας Ἀτρείδας
> δάκρυ μὴ κατασχεῖν·   (202–3)

The effect is one of emotional outburst: the agitated feelings give a violent climax to the strophe. In the strophe we see the anguish of the Atridae at the cruel prophecy; in the antistrophe, the almost fierce determination of Agamemnon not only to accept but desire the sacrifice:

> παυσανέμου γὰρ
> θυσίας παρθενίου θ' αἵματος ὀργᾷ
> περιόργως ἐπιθυμεῖν
> θέμις. εὖ γὰρ εἴη.'   (214–17)

The mood of resigned acceptance indicated by the last trochaic antistrophe (184–92) has passed to one of anguish and self-hypnosis. We see the plight of the impotent expedition, the terrible ship-destroying calm, the violent reaction of the chiefs to the suggested remedy, the passion of Agamemnon's response.

The next pair of strophes (218–37) takes up the "strained" iambs once more (ἐπεὶ δ' ἀνάγκας ἔδυ λέπαδνον, 218) and indeed repeats the pattern three times (219, 221, 222, 228–29, and 231–32 in the antistrophe) but varies it by a burst of emotional shorts: ἄναγνον,

3. *Greek Lyric Meter* (Cambridge, 1929) 108.

ἀνίερον, τόθεν (220); and ἔτλα δ᾽ οὖν θυτὴρ γενέσθαι τάλαινα παρακοπὰ πρωτοπήμων. ἔτλα δ᾽ οὖν. (224). The succession of the shorts by the three bacchii of 224 is a particularly impressive contrast. The end of this strophe is not emotional in the manner of the preceding section (continuous choriambs) but is marked by a choriamb in each line, which breaks the strain and emotion with a sort of ironic finality. "This was the sacrifice required by the war to avenge the loss of a promiscuous woman: this was how he kept his daughter from emitting an ominous word!" (225–27; 235–37).

These strophes describe the result of Agamemnon's fierce determination. When he accepted the yoke of necessity, his nature changed: the change was impious, unholy (δυσσεβῆ τροπάιαν / ἄναγνον ἀνίερον, 219–20). It was ill-counseled (αἰσχρόμητις, 222), wretched infatuation (τάλαινα παρακοπὰ πρωτοπήμων, 223). The pathetic scene of the sacrifice underlines the horror of the deed: Iphigenia had to be gagged in order to prevent her uttering a fatal curse. Here is the other side of Agamemnon's obedience to Zeus that was described in the last trochaic antistrophe. He now passionately desires to make this sacrifice; his whole nature is altered. This is his guilt. The passage is the climax of the long parodos.

(e) The last section (238–57) rounds off and closes the parodos. The first strophe continues the account of the sacrifice, run over from the preceding antistrophe. The preceding "strained" iambs (e.g., 193, 218) are slightly toned down by ending with a cretic rather than a bacchius (βίᾳ χαλινῶν δ᾽, ἀναύδῳ μένει, 238) as opposed to, e.g., 206: (βαρεῖα μὲν κὴρ τὸ μὴ πιθέσθαι). The result is a less stressful or more regular verse (two iambs, two cretics). Emotion is beginning to subside. The chorus does not see the sequel of the sacrifice and will not tell it. Yet Justice will still weigh out its lesson to those who suffer (τοῖς μὲν παθοῦσιν, 250). The future will be what it will be. To greet in advance is to mourn in advance. The final hope is for εὐπραξις (255), a happy result. That hope, in the context of the whole parodos, seems dim indeed.

Aeschylus has now established the context for Agamemnon's return. The abrupt transition at the end of the parodos from past to future corresponds to the mixture of past and present in the opening anapaests. The old men of the chorus are describing the basis of their forebodings, the point of view from which they see the impending end of the war and Agamemnon's return. He is the righteous avenger of Paris' misdeed and the guilty slayer of Iphigenia, but he is also the object of divine necessity, subject to the teaching and power of Zeus. The war is both just and unjust, a righteous response to Paris' misdeed and a fatal sacrifice of an innocent for an evil woman. Weal and woe, bad and good, justice

and guilt, are inextricably mingled. There is no way of interpreting this parodos so that its ambiguity can be clarified. The
future—the drama to come—and only the future can do this. As
yet, nothing has been said of the house of Atreus and its chain of
crimes and vengeance. There is an allusion to the child-avenging
Wrath (Menis, 155) that we know is Clytemnestra's; the watchman
has darkly hinted of evil things in the palace; but we are as yet
concerned only with war, and the guilt of Agamemnon in it.

The importance of this point has been underestimated in most
commentary on the play. Something is not good about the war,
despite its righteous cause. This evil or unhealthiness is centered
on the two women concerned, on Helen and Iphigenia. The words

$$ἔτλα δ' οὖν θυτὴρ γενέσθαι$$
$$θυγατρός, γυναικοποίνων$$
$$πολέμων ἀρωγὰν$$
$$καὶ προτέλεια ναῶν \qquad (224–27)$$

are bitterly ironical. The expedition was sent by Zeus Xenios in
behalf of the justly aggrieved Atridae (the bereft vultures), but it
was nonetheless a terrible struggle in the interest of a promiscuous
woman (πολυάνορος ἀμφὶ γυναικός, 62). It was not only that Agamemnon had sacrificed his daughter. The dire necessity is recognized, and that necessity is one of the play's premises. Nothing
in the parodos is more vivid or convincing than Agamemnon's
anguish at the necessity. But Agamemnon is guilty. His guilt is
dependent on the attitude that he came to take toward this necessity. At first he seemed to accept it as part of Zeus' χάρις (182), or
wisdom. Later he added to his acceptance a fierce personal complicity. This guilt tainted the whole war. What Agamemnon has
done at Troy is what the eagles have done to the hare, an indul-
gence in inhumanity and cruelty, a lack of humane perspective, a
change in the character of a good king and father. Iphigenia's
sacrifice is a symbol and a cause. We await Agamemnon's return in
a mood of great uncertainty: can we rejoice in his victory without
regard to his war-guilt? This consideration will later be merged in
the problem of the guilt of his house, of divine responsibility for
his and its actions. Yet for the moment, the question of his war-
guilt takes the upper hand.

Even here the ambiguity of the parodos is evident. The watchman has indicated that it is not the events at Troy but the evil
deeds of Argos' present rulers (Clytemnestra and Aegisthus), the
things that palace walls could utter if they had voice, which cloud
the joy of Agamemnon's victory and his prospective return. Calchas' reference to the terrible child-avenging treacherous Wrath

(δολία μνάμων μῆνις τεκνόποινος, 155) that will abide in the house of Atreus as a result of Iphigenia's sacrifice connects this foreboding with Clytemnestra's desire for vengeance. Agamemnon's woe, the thing that will cloud his victory, and bring his guilt home to him, is not at Troy but at Argos. That the chorus can only speak of his Trojan guilt (his war-guilt), that Iphigenia's sacrifice is connected with this rather than Clytemnestra herself, that the evil woman referred to is Helen, not Clytemnestra—are all evidence of the fear and the enforced silence that obscure their words. The connection (referred to by the watchman) between faraway Troy and the Argive palace immediately beneath, is close, yet for that very reason deliberately obscured.

The nature of the war and the guilt of Agamemnon cast a shadow upon his victory, but this shadow has not as yet reached the point of total eclipse. Precisely because the designs of Clytemnestra are as yet unfulfilled—Agamemnon has been shamed by her adulterous acts, not brutally killed—the main burden of guilt has not yet shifted to her. The chorus shows less obvious devotion to its expected lord or master than the watchman, being much more concerned with Agamemnon's guilt, but it would be wrong to interpret its attitude as one of opposition to him. It is loyal and respectful even if doubtful and confused. It knows that Zeus teaches wisdom by suffering but it does not know what that wisdom is or can be.

(3) The first episode (264–354) is short but highly suggestive; it is a preview of the succeeding episode of the herald, a dramatic presentation of the general ambiguity of the play before the murder, a first revelation of Clytemnestra's character, and a new hint of the dark domestic background of Agamemnon's return. The chorus is skeptical of the beacons. It shows no awareness of Clytemnestra's intelligence and bold initiative. She herself is hard put to contain her elation at the prospect of approaching vengeance. Her two long speeches—the vivid account of the beacons, the equally vivid imaginary picture of the captured Troy—convey, in masterpieces of double meaning, the full force of her masculine energy and ferocious duplicity. The account of the beacon fires (281–316) splendidly develops the motif of light. Her horrible joy at the news reaches its height in her proclamation of the coming of light to Argos:

> κἄπειτ᾽ Ἀτρειδῶν ἐς τόδε σκήπτει στέγος
> φάος τόδ᾽ οὐκ ἄπαππον Ἰδαίου πυρός.
> τοιοίδε τοί μοι λαμπαδηφόρων νομοί,

> ἄλλος παρ' ἄλλου διαδοχαῖς πληρούμενοι·
> νικᾷ δ' ὁ πρῶτος καὶ τελευταῖος δραμών.   (310–14)

What will strike at Argos is light to her heart, akin to the light of burning Troy. But the chorus is still skeptical (317–19). Clytemnestra first pictures the blended cries and cares of victors and vanquished. Her ostensible joy for the former barely conceals her hope for their destruction:

> ἔρως δὲ μή τις πρότερον ἐμπίπτῃ στρατῷ
> πορθεῖν ἃ μὴ χρή, κέρδεσιν νικωμένους.
> δεῖ γὰρ πρὸς οἴκους νοστίμου σωτηρίας
> κάμψαι διαύλου θάτερον κῶλον πάλιν·
> θεοῖς δ' ἀναμπλάκητος εἰ μόλοι στρατός,
> ἐγρηγορὸς τὸ πῆμα τῶν ὀλωλότων
> γένοιτ' ἄν, εἰ πρόσπαιά πῃ τεύχοι κακά.   (341–47)

So, as before, the ominous danger of the victory—the eagles' fatal banquet once again—is brought out, but in a hypocritical disguise. The chorus seems to accept these clear proofs (πιστά σου τεκμήρια, 352), though its doubt is not dissipated, as its later words reveal.

(4) The point of departure of the stasimon is the victory itself, while the parodos was centered on the ominous departure of the Greek army. Starting with the divine justification of Troy's defeat, the initial twelve anapaests (355–66) describe the defeat as the closing of a dragnet on the evil city. Zeus Xenios has finally completed his vengeance on Paris.

The net motif—which is akin to the yoke of necessity that descended upon Agamemnon at Aulis—directs the fluctuations of human guilt and divine necessity. Both Paris or Troy and Agamemnon are caught in the net; each alternately shares the same sense of guilt and the same fate; the transition from one to the other is constantly occurring. We can note the same fluctuation in Aeschylus' use of the bird (vultures and eagles), lion (second stasimon), and snake (*Choephoroe*) motifs. Here the net motif itself does not shift from Paris to Agamemnon, but as we shall see, the incidents and emphasis of the whole stasimon shift from the one to the other, so that what is said of Paris becomes applicable to Agamemnon or the Atridae. The fluidity that we have noticed in the parodos is more evident here. It determines the movement of the strophes. This fluidity or changing of sides is the opposite of the recurrence of themes we find in "ring composition."

The lyrics begin with Paris and his fate. Their metrical construction differs from that of the parodos. The three sets of strophes (the last with an epode) are basically similar: relatively "unstrained" iambics with a glyconic-pherecratean refrain at the end of each strophe. Thus the opening lines of the first strophe,

> Διὸς πλαγὰν ἔχουσιν εἰπεῖν,
> πάρεστιν τοῦτό γ' ἐξιχνεῦσαι.
> ἔπραξεν ὡς ἔκρανεν. οὐκ ἔφα τις
> θεοὺς βροτῶν ἀξιοῦσθαι μέλειν
> ὅσοις ἀθίκτων χάρις
> πατοῖθ'· ὁ δ' οὐκ εὐσεβής,   (367–72)

do not really strain the iambic movement. Even in 370, θεοὺς βροτῶν ἀξιοῦσθαι μέλειν, the paired cretics at the end maintain a regularity that compensates for the shift from pure iambic rhythm after the fourth foot. The five "choriambic" lines at the end of each strophe (e.g., 380–84) provide a pleasant finality. The first pair of strophes deals with a past event—the deserved fate of Paris. They show the results of impiety—of trampling on sacred or untouchable things—and its cause, the pride produced by excessive wealth. Wretched Peitho (Persuasion), child of Infatuation (Ate), persuades the crime that brings the violent end. There is no help: the base bronze will be judged and seen in its own gleaming blackness. The boy who foolishly chases the flying bird will ultimately bring ruin on his city. The gods will destroy him. Such was Paris.

The first antistrophe brings in a new element in its last line: Paris dishonored the hospitality of the Atridae by the theft of a wife (ᾔσχυνε ξενίαν τράπε- / ζαν κλοπαῖσι γυναικός, 401–2). So the next pair of strophes are concerned solely with Helen. First we see the loneliness of Menelaus, his empty bed, his inability to take pleasure in the shapely statues of his palace. Only an empty phantom of love is left. These two strophes make a transition (in the antistrophe): such were things at home (τὰ μὲν κατ' οἴκους ἐφ' ἑστίας ἄχη, 427); they were otherwise with the people of Greece, who endured the war without overt grief but with much that touched their heart, for of the men that they had sent off to war, there came back only urns and ashes.

The final pair of strophes are concerned with the war, the war dead, and the feelings of their kin at home. The Atridae as the authors of the war are the objects of whispered resentment: the people pronounce a curse upon them. Nor are the gods unmindful of those who cause so many to die. In time the dark Erinyes will reverse the fortune of the unjustly prosperous man. Zeus' thunderbolt will fall on him when he is praised to excess. The chorus ends with a hope for unveiled prosperity, to be neither a taker of cities nor the taken.

Once more, then, the guilt of Agamemnon and of the Atridae has come to the fore. Particularly notable is the ambivalence of the ode. The guilt of the Trojans and the justification of the Atridae— their wielding of the great dragnet against their wicked enemies— are subtly succeeded by the reverse, the guilt of the Atridae themselves and the justification of those who murmur against them. The ominous victim of the gods' wrath is at first Paris himself; then the chorus turns to Helen and from her to Menelaus, her own victim in the amatory sense; at this point they turn again with an insidiously rapid shift in emphasis to the Argive people, whose real animus is directed not against Troy or Paris but against Menelaus and Agamemnon. This animus is justified: the last words of the ode associate them with the wicked rich man who had been identified with Paris. This war for a woman is their fault; they have sinned through excessive prosperity and fatal adulation. The dark Erinyes will wear them down and destroy them. All this is couched in deliberate obscurity. The important point is the ambivalence, the almost bewildering ambiguity of the ode and its all but complete identification of the personal guilt of Agamemnon or the Atridae with the war-guilt as such. There even seems to be a faintly pacifist strain in the final remarks of the chorus, a condemnation of all war.

Both sides are at fault, and a morality that condemns one inevitably condemns the other. But there is a difference of guilts and of characters, which the chorus recognizes. The guilt of Paris and Helen is clearer and greater than that of the Atridae. Yet the chorus had not yet learned to discriminate guilt with any clarity. On a poetical level the fluidity of the argument—the insidious shift from Paris to Agamemnon—is the primary organizing principle of the stasimon. But poetical movement and movement of content go hand in hand. The ambiguity or fluidity not only increases the connotative force of the language; it is essential to the drama itself.

(5) The second episode (503–680) confirms the ambiguity of the preceding episode and stasimon. Victory and ruinous storm, weal and woe, human triumph and divine punishment, are again juxtaposed. But the juxtaposition is clearer, more ominous, and underlined by an ironic contrast of appearance and reality. Clytemnestra's hypocritical delight in Agamemnon's announced return corresponds to the herald's naive pleasure in the ill-fated triumph. Again the light motif is prominent: ἥκει γὰρ ὑμῖν φῶς ἐν

εὐφρόνῃ φέρων (522), referring to Agamemnon. The yoke motif is repeated (τοιόνδε Τροίᾳ περιβαλὼν ζευκτήριον ἄναξ Ἀτρείδης, 529–30). The destruction of Troy is proclaimed with ominous hyperbole, in a particularly dire metaphor: καὶ σπέρμα πάσης ἐξαπόλλυται χθονός (528). We recall the eagles and the pregnant hare. The herald does not understand the enigmatic language of the chorus (524–28)—its chronic remedy for its woes has ever been silence or the "silence" of enigmatic language (πάλαι τὸ σιγᾶν φάρμακον βλάβης ἔχω, 548). He takes its announced desire for death (550) simply as a sign of supreme happiness—i.e., there is nothing to wish for after such success. He contrasts the Greek hardships at Troy with the joy of the achievement that those hardships have made possible. All is due to the grace of Zeus: καὶ χάρις τιμήσεται / Διὸς τάδ᾽ ἐκπράξασα (581–82).

The entrance of Clytemnestra shifts the tone and meaning of the scene. She begins with a deliberate recall of the cry of joy with which she greeted the beacons: ἀνωλόλυξα μὲν πάλαι χαρᾶς ὕπο (587). She pointedly reproves the skepticism of the chorus. They can now see the justification of her womanly credulity. She needs no information from the herald; she will soon have it from Agamemnon. All she wants to convey now is her loyalty and devotion to him. Her hypocrisy and irony are deliberately intensified: she welcomes Agamemnon as the "city's favorite" (ἐράσμιον πόλει, 605). There is no light sweeter to her than him. She has been his faithful watchdog, his sealed vessel. All rumors of adultery—she boldly proclaims the truth in reverse—are false coin. She boasts of her purity and excuses the shame of her boasts.

Her quick departure leaves the chorus and the herald in a decidedly uneasy confrontation. Such hypocrisy cannot be left without comment. The chorus must say something. As before, the chorus will only hint at the truth. Clytemnestra's words, it says, are fair (εὐπρεπῶς, 616) if rightly interpreted. Then it turns (with obvious deliberateness) from this unwelcome subject to another which turns out to be even more unwelcome: what is the news of Menelaus? Is he also safe? This introduces the other side of the herald's message: the woes of the Greeks' return. He has a blend of good and bad to tell: πῶς κεδνὰ τοῖς κακοῖσι συμμείξω (648); a paean of the Erinyes is mixed with his news of salvation. The sea has blossomed with the corpses of the returning Achaeans. (The metaphor is a crowning instance of the conversion of fair into foul, natural into unnatural, that characterizes Aeschylus' language and illustrates that fluidity of motif—the changing of sides or the shifting of a motif's applicability—which is characteristic of the whole play.) The fate of Menelaus is unknown but Savior Luck (τύχη δὲ σωτήρ, 664) has preserved Agamemnon. A god, no man, had his hand on the tiller of the ship. The ominousness of this apparently divine intervention on Agamemnon's behalf is brought out when we are told the real reason for the fatal storm that has been so destructive of the Greeks' homecoming. It is nothing less than the wrath of the gods themselves: χειμὼν᾽ Ἀχαιῶν οὐκ ἀμήνιτον θεοῖς (649). The suggestion of Clytemnestra—that the Greeks would incur the gods' wrath by their impious destruction of Troy and its temples—has been validated. There is something pointed in the gods' deliberate safeguarding of Agamemnon. They have saved him for another fate. The clear implication is that he deserves it. He, like the other returning Greeks, was guilty of impiety, to which Aeschylus adds an equally disturbing inhumanity.

The naive obtuseness of the herald—who does not know what has been going on at Argos and takes only the surface view of the war and the shipwreck—produces a highly ironic effect. It is the shipwreck (Helen, the ship-destroyer), not the victory, that inspires the beginning of the next stasimon. The victory has already been discounted by the chorus.

(6) The second stasimon (681–781 followed by anapaests of greeting to Agamemnon, 782–809) is not concerned solely with the shipwreck; it is designed to precede Agamemnon's deliberately pompous entrance. It deals with the war that is now more than ever on everyone's mind—but with a curiously accentuated pessimism. The woes are uppermost and the stasimon's moral, though ostensibly directed at Helen rather than Paris or the Atridae, is applicable to Agamemnon. The movement of the stasimon is indicated by three major shifts of the meter. The first strophe and antistrophe start with trochees, develop into impassioned choriambs and minor ionics, and close with lower-keyed glyconics and pherecrateans. The moment of passion comes with the play on Helen's name—ἑλέναυς, ἕλανδρος, ἑλέπτολις (688)—or in the antistrophe with the wedding song, the ὑμέναιον (707) that becomes a hymn of woe (ὕμνον . . . πολύθρηνον, 709–11). Helen is well named the ship-wrecker or city-wrecker. Her marriage song that dishonors Zeus Xenios is soon unlearned by the Trojans that sing it. It becomes only a hymn of woe like the marriage (κῆδος ὀρθώνυμον, 699–700)—that is, as the double meaning of the word suggests, a woe indeed. This introduction, based on Helen's name and the double meaning of κῆδος at 699 (woe, marriage), leads to a quieter pair of strophes: glyconics, semihexameters, trochaics (that begin with shorts), and concluding glyconic-pherecratean lines.

They tell the story of the lion cub, first the darling and pet of the family, then growing into a veritable priest of Ate that devours the household. The obvious moral is developed in a pair of different strophes, more like the first, but this time beginning with "strained" or "syncopated" iambs, passing into animated minor ionics, and again closing with two glyconic-pherecratean lines. Helen was the darling lion that became the evil Erinys of the household. This moral is expanded in the antistrophe with a rather different and more inclusive application. There was an old saying that a man's prosperity does not die childless but begets woe for his race out of his good fortune. The chorus pointedly demurs:

> δίχα δ' ἄλλων μονόφρων εἰ-
> μί. τὸ δυσσεβὲς γὰρ ἔργον
> μετὰ μὲν πλείονα τίκτει,
> σφετέρᾳ δ' εἰκότα γέννᾳ.
> οἴκων γὰρ εὐθυδίκων
> καλλίπαις πότμος ἀεί.   (757–62)

An evil deed begets others like itself, but this is not true of houses that keep true justice (οἴκων εὐθυδίκων, 761). Justice is not an inevitable consequence of prosperity.

The transition is clear and significant. The simile of the household lion is applicable to any evil person. (We shall see that Helen vies with Clytemnestra as the evil woman of Argos and the Greeks.) Again we note the fluidity of reference—the shift of sides—just as in the preceding stasimon and parodos. It is evil itself that dooms the household. The good husband—and presumably the good individual (though he is not particularly distinguished from his household)—is immune. The last two strophes of the stasimon in general carry out the "strained" iambic meter of the preceding pair of strophes, as in

> φιλεῖ δὲ τίκτειν "Υβρις
> μὲν παλαιὰ νεά-
> ζουσαν ἐν κακοῖς βροτῶν
> "Υβριν τότ' ἢ τόθ'   (763–66)

where a succession of four cretics interrupt the initial iambic feet, but they add a significant final word. Old *hybris* is wont to breed a bold new *daimon* against which all resistance is useless, a black Ate resembling her progenetrix. Justice after all shines (λάμπει, 772) in smoky cottages rather than in gilded mansions. She does not revere the power of wealth, even when it is falsely praised.

As in the preceding stasimon, the ostensible target is the ob-

viously wicked person, here Helen, as there Paris. But here, as
there, the target wavers and shifts. The lesson goes beyond Helen
or Paris. The chorus, despite the obscurity of its reference, is
extending its view to the house of Atreus itself. Helen is closer to
home than Paris. It was not only Troy that had experienced excessive prosperity. There is an easy and ominous transition from
Troy to Argos. Unlike the preceding stasimon, here the Atridae
are not specifically mentioned. The war-guilt has been a prevailing
theme since the parodos and could figure in the preceding (second)
stasimon, but the house of Atreus has not yet emerged into the
open save in the most enigmatic hints of the watchman and the
even more enigmatic silence of the chorus. The second stasimon
prepares the way for its emergence. The mysterious recurrence of
crime in a household, its connection with the *dike* of Zeus, with
the wealth and the *hybris* of the great, with the doubtful possibility
of an escape from such dangers are suggested. Troy is dead and
gone but its lesson remains for Argos. It is time for such a re-
minder: Agamemnon himself enters as the stasimon ends, and the
coincidence is intentional. Though his entrance now carries with
it a new concern for himself and his ancestry—his position in
Argos—he is still a hero and ultimately the man guilty of the war.

Can we not, even so, take Agamemnon as a prosperous but good
man whom the chorus has pointedly mentioned as immune from
the fate of the bad? Do the last two strophes really cancel this
application of the moral? We cannot answer definitely, for any
definiteness at this point would destroy the fluidity or ambiguity
that Aeschylus wanted. There is more to Agamemnon's guilt than
mere excess of prosperity: if he is not bad, he is not simply good.
Otherwise the previous parodos and stasima would be wholly
irrelevant. On the other hand, the wickedness of Helen does seem
to have overtones that apply to Clytemnestra. But Clytemnestra is
not as yet the simply guilty to be opposed to the predominantly
innocent. There is a *hybris* in Agamemnon that the ensuing episode
will bring out; when Clytemnestra persuades him to walk the
tapestry she is forcing him to exhibit it. The change came over
him at Aulis, the new nature he acquired there is still with him.
But it would be a great mistake to view him as a merely bad or evil
person.

(7) Agamemnon now enters in his chariot. Cassandra is with
him but probably less prominently placed in the rear of the vehicle.
The chorus speaks to him in anapaests, which are part of the
episode, not of the preceding stasimon, but which are still envel-

oped in a quasi-lyric obscurity. The deliberate refusal of these old Argives to flatter him or praise imposing arrival is striking. How can they honor him as he deserves?

The question is important because there has already been so much hypocrisy. So many (the reference to Clytemnestra is obvious) prefer appearance (τὸ δοκεῖν εἶναι, 788) to the reality of the true *dike*. The difference between flattery (σαίνειν, 798) and true friendship is now crucial. This is why the chorus boldly expresses its own reservations to Agamemnon's conduct of the war. Its picture of Agamemnon was indeed sour (κάρτ' ἀπομούσως ἦσθα γεγραμμένος, 801) when he led off the army, all for the sake of that woman, Helen. He was not then a wise ruler (οὐδ' εὖ πραπίδων οἴακα νέμων, 802). But matters are now (νῦν δ', 805) different: its friendship is now no lip service (οὐκ ἀπ' ἄκρας φρενός, 805). As for others in Argos, he will learn in time who are just and who are not. Here the notable thing is not the reservations but the loyalty of the chorus. The elders express their loyalty by their reservations, their very frankness. They remain faithful to Agamemnon in spite if his war-guilt. Between him and Clytemnestra they have no choice at all: the one is their good and just king, the other an evil hypocrite. And there is the yet unmentioned Aegisthus.

This anapaestic passage is important since it throws considerable light on the parodos and preceding stasima. To the chorus, Agamemnon is not a simple innocent without guilt. But there has been considerable ambiguity in their conception of his guilt. They recognize the rightness of his acts as the agent of Zeus Xenios, the divine avenger of profaned hospitality. They do not blame him for the necessity of the sacrifice of Iphigenia. Nevertheless they cannot approve of this war for an evil woman. Something went wrong and they see its origin in the fatal change that came over Agamemnon when he not only accepted but oddly desired the dreadful sacrifice at Aulis. But all this is past: the present (νῦν δ') is what concerns them. They are unable to see how the will of Zeus and *dike* can be fulfilled, but Agamemnon is their true representative at Argos. They are only too glad to look upon his war-guilt as a thing of the past.

Agamemnon's introductory speech is addressed first to the gods (820–29) and second to the chorus itself (830–50) and closes with four brief lines stating that he will now go to his palace and hearth and sacrifice to the gods who have given him victory. His address to the gods can only be looked upon as arrogant.[4] He sees no

---

4. But see Eduard Fraenkel, *Aeschylus "Agamemnon,"* vol. 2 (Oxford, 1950) *ad* 811, pp. 371–74.

problem in the complete destruction of Troy, no difference of viewpoint between the gods and himself. The language of such lines as

> καπνῷ δ' ἁλοῦσα νῦν ἔτ' εὔσημος πόλις.
> ἄτης θύελλαι ζῶσι· συνθνήσκουσα δὲ
> σποδὸς προπέμπει πίονας πλούτου πνοάς.
> τούτων θεοῖσι χρὴ πολύμνηστον χάριν
> τίνειν, ἐπείπερ χάρπαγὰς ὑπερκόπους
> ἐπραξάμεσθα καὶ γυναικὸς οὕνεκα
> πόλιν διημάθυνεν Ἀργεῖον δάκος,
> ἵππου νεοσσός, ἀσπιδηφόρος λεώς,
> πήδημ' ὀρούσας ἀμφὶ Πλειάδων δύσιν·
> ὑπερθορὼν δὲ πύργον ὠμηστὴς λέων
> ἄδην ἔλειξεν αἵματος τυραννικοῦ.   (818–28)

identifies Agamemnon himself and the Greeks with many of the sinister motifs of the play (the lion, 827, and the snake, 834) and twists the good motifs (especially the innocent young ἵππου νεοσσός, 825) into a sinister meaning. He is not the right man to speak of ravening (ὠμηστὴς, 827) beasts licking up the blood of princes or of the rich aroma of wealth (πίονας πλούτου πνοάς, 820) that blows from the embers of the city totally destroyed. Again we note the fluidity of motif, the way in which foul becomes fair and fair foul. The shifting here is the work of Agamemnon and an index of his culpability. He is the harsh general, the changed man of the parodos. His subsequent words to the chorus reveal a different aspect of his character. He does not arrogantly reject their frankness (as such a king might well have done) but invites them to counsel with him on affairs at Argos. He appreciates the rarity of true friends. The whole speech is intensely ironic: Agamemnon's moral platitudes are turned against him; even the gods are his enemies, not his friends. He has come home too late for anything but his death. His speech ends with his announced intention to thank his household gods for his victory!

The entrance of Clytemnestra shifts our sympathies toward Agamemnon. His guilt may be ambivalent; hers is repulsively evident. Adulation as fulsome as that which she heaps upon her intended victim, hypocrisy so gross, are the dramatically essential means of differentiating the good from the bad. Agamemnon has just agreed with the chorus about the rarity of honest friendship and the envy and flattery that follow men of good fortune. To these sentiments, Clytemnestra's words are counterpoised with effective irony. She seems to have a compulsive urge to flatter by suggesting the truth, to pick out the salient facts and invert just them, to display her intentions in highly topical and predictive metaphor. She dwells on the misery of sitting at home without a man, the reports of Agamemnon's death that came thick as the meshes in a net, her desire to save Orestes by sending him away from a popular revolution, her fear of the Argive people because it is in their nature to kick a man who is down (τὸν πεσόντα λακτίσαι, 885), her inability to sleep in Agamemnon's absence; every word she says is either an inversion of the terrible past or a suggestion of the terrible future. Here, once more, fair is made foul, but in a different way from the speech of Agamemnon, whose *hybris* is in no sense hypocritical and whose chief virtue (as here displayed) is a frank honesty of utterance.

The climax of the scene—the significant action that gives dramatic force to her words—is the spreading of the tapestries. His path is to be spread with them, she says, so that *dike* herself may lead him to the home to which he has beyond expectation returned. The double meaning is plain enough: to her he is a righteous victim, and his death must pay for that of Iphigenia; publicly he is the righteous conqueror of wicked Troy, a paladin of justice. By making him walk on such costly splendor, she is treating him like Pride before its inevitable fall and inducing him to exhibit a *hybris* like that of Xerxes flogging the sea or, more particularly, like the boastful rich man of the preceding stasimon. The tapestries are a symbol, but Agamemnon's acceptance of the symbol gives it a sort of liturgical power. He has cooperated in his own destruction.

He does not cooperate without some show of resistance. His tone toward Clytemnestra is one of scarcely concealed disdain. Her speech, he says, has been well suited to his absence, for both have been excessively long. Praise such as hers should come only from others. He finds her whole approach repulsive. His attitude toward her is comprehensible; we know what Clytemnestra is like. But the sheer folly of such coldness and disdain in a man returning home, with the blood of his and her daughter on his hands and his captured concubine at his side, is all but staggering. He oddly mistakes the character of Clytemnestra. He regards the tapestries as an act of womanish folly. She does not, he thinks, see that such effeminate pampering puts him on the level of an eastern monarch, makes him the mark of envy from the gods, and pays to a mortal honor that has been reserved for them. Tapestries are one thing; carpets another. To tread on the first is an act of presumption like her indiscriminate praise. Praise is only safe when a man has concluded his life in prosperity. Agamemnon is here indulging in platitudes he lacks the will to heed, and which are ironically turned against him.

If he has correctly but blindly gauged the intention of Clytemnestra's act—she does indeed want him to look like an infatuated mortal exciting the envy of men and gods—he fails to penetrate her character or her feelings. He treats the past as if it did not exist or count. He is not taken in by her hypothetical cases or her appeal to his pride. But he is not much interested in prolonging the argument. Can victory in such a contest, he asks, mean all that much to her? To which she replies, πιθοῦ· κρατεῖς μέντοι παρεὶς ἑκὼν ἐμοί (943). He can best show his superiority by his voluntary compliance; at which he yields, saying, "Ah well, if that is what you want" (ἀλλ' εἰ δοκεῖ σοι ταῦθ', 944).

He has no idea of the true situation and has exhibited a peculiarly devastating combination of insensitivity and weakness. The impression he gives is one of faint annoyance at Clytemnestra's feminine persistence, an annoyance which indicates that he is not prepared to make a fuss, for she is really not worth it. The weak compromise of removing his shoes will under the circumstances have to suffice. He cares so little for her feelings that he can even commend Cassandra to her attention and can compound the insult by a little platitude on the duty of the powerful to their slaves. He goes off stating that since he has been reduced to compliance, he will "enter the palace treading on the purple" (957).

As he goes, Clytemnestra indulges in one more masterpiece of hypocrisy and double meaning. Who can ever drain the sea of its purple? There is enough, and more than enough, for the dyeing of vestments. The house of Atreus is not poor. She would have vowed many robes for him to tread on if an oracle had commanded that way of insuring his return. He is her shade in summer, her warmth in winter, a coolness at the time when Zeus makes wine from the sour grape. Her murderous delight is here so close to ecstasy that the hypocritical language reveals her real emotion. She follows him in after a brief and wholly sincere appeal to Zeus the Fulfiller (Ζεῦ Ζεῦ τέλειε, 973) to accomplish her prayers and his own divine intent.

The scene is perfect in its combination of arrogance, weakness, hypocrisy, and hardly contained exaltation. Agamemnon's character is such that one can feel no pity for him even as he walks to his doom. He is not the man who once rejoiced in the clear voice of his daughter in the banquet hall. He seems devoid of human quality. His weakness before Clytemnestra is the result of his ignorance even more than of his insensitivity. To the chorus, who have more insight and understanding than he, the scene is ominous. Yet the chorus does not act; it feels only a vague dread, a dim premonition of woe and death. It now combines its persistent ambiguity with a lack of all hope.

(8) The third stasimon (975–1033) reflects this mood. It starts with a pair of strophes in which solemn trochees break into a line of dactyls as the fluttering terror in the hearts of the chorus finds expression. What is the dread they feel? The war has gone by—time has passed since the sand flew from the loosened cables of the departing Greek ships—and the chorus has seen their return with its own eyes. Why then this dirge, this loveless self-taught dirge, that an Erinys sings within them? Such premonition cannot be vain—the heart and mind show the working of an obscure justice; they sway in "eddies of fulfillment," an uneasy sense that retribution is at hand. The chorus hopes the forebodings will prove false. A man (Agamemnon is implied) can perhaps save himself by jettisoning the wealth that displeases the gods, avoid the hidden reef, and save the ship. But there is no retrieving blood that has once been spilt, for Zeus forbids it. If the chorus's share of divine spirit were not limited by fate ($\mu o \hat{\iota} \rho a$, 1026), its heart would outrun its tongue and pour out the truth. As it is, it is enveloped in darkness and without hope of carrying out any timely purpose, much as its heart may burn.

Although this chorus is enigmatic, and its enigma is increased for modern readers by the unreliability of the text, the basic meaning seems clear enough. The chorus has a premonition of impending woe, of woe in the form of just retribution. This is no ordinary terror that can be remedied by a process of lightening the ship, divesting oneself of an envied prosperity. There is bloodshed—irretrievable death—at hand, though the darkness forbids clear vision. The chorus obscurely foresees the murder of Agamemnon and obscurely recognizes its justice, despite reluctance to do so. The guilt it has harped on, for all its ambiguity, has now come to the point of paying the final retributive penalty. Yet there is horror and dread in the prospect. Now less than ever does the chorus desire such an outcome or such a justice. It has no wish to see a return even more terrible and joyless than the setting out. Despite this wish, woe has finally won the victory over weal.

The long Cassandra scene (1035–1330), of almost three hundred lines, comes as contrast and climax to the preceding episodes and stasima. We no longer remain in the dim, ambiguous, gropingly moralistic thought-world of the chorus. The guilt of Agamemnon is no longer the problem. The war itself is over and done with. There is no question any more of Agamemnon's fate; that is decided. Even the chorus cannot conceal its terrible if obscure conviction. But the moment of doom is held back, so that a final and different interpretation of Agamemnon's destiny can emerge. Between Agamemnon's and Cassandra's exits into the palace comes the revelation of the demon or Erinys of the house of Atreus.

The chorus does not realize the bearing of this revelation on Agamemnon himself. They are still human, without the gift of prophecy, and barred by the peculiar fate of Cassandra from understanding even her clearest words. The very impregnability of their ignorance enhances their ultimate surprise. Aeschylus has no interest in mere surprise. The Cassandra scene conveys the sensation of doom in the making, doom inevitable and yet mysteriously suspended, doom foreseen and accepted, and yet held off by a limited moment of revelation, of prophetic delay uncannily prolonged.

Even before Clytemnestra appears beside the two corpses, the past has been summed up, the future anticipated, the real problem of the play made visible and, by its visibility, put in the way of its solution. The murder is decisive because it stands at a decisive moment in time, a moment which Cassandra has stopped until its meaning can be seen. The Cassandra episode is the climax of the play, the scene that extends and heightens the climax to an almost unbearable intensity.

The great event of the trilogy is not the murder but the fateful shift from an old to a new condition of things. Up to that last stasimon, the chorus was concerned with Agamemnon and Troy, its attention straying in unresolved ambiguity from the guilt of the Trojans (Paris especially) to that of the Atridae, and particularly the guilt of Agamemnon. The war—especially the departure and return of the Greeks, summed up in Agamemnon's departure and return—had involved both sides in its evil, as had the ominous Helen, elevated by the chorus to a symbol of their dual, shared guilt. The chorus did not deny the justice of Troy's punishment or equate the two guilts. Its sympathies were not with Clytemnestra, even though it had refused to express them except by deliberately emphasized "silence." Its primary concern was with the dreadful ambiguity that surrounded Agamemnon's return. This could not be a joyous event as victory and homecoming would normally be, because the whole war and Agamemnon's part in it had been too deeply involved in guilt and therefore subject to the retribution that the final stasimon so reluctantly suggests. Woe had from the start reduced weal or joy to a mere ghost of itself, and at the end (third stasimon) had quite overcome it. The war had been justified, in the eyes of both men and gods, but it had lost its innocence ever since that fatal change in Agamemnon's character when he took on the guilt as well as the divine necessity of killing his own daughter. All this was part of the old dispensation, from which the chorus could see no easy or satisfactory outcome.

Now the retribution—which the chorus sees as an inevitable and irretrievable "spilling of blood"—is at hand. Cassandra takes it for granted (the possibility of changing, even deferring Agamemnon's and her own fate is never contemplated), and the placement of her scene *before* the murder is a device for enhancing the sense of doom, of penultimate prophecy, so that the gods seem present and prophecy and event are merged in an unnatural and horribly distended present. The question is no longer one of Agamemnon's guilt or of the war in whose perspective his guilt has so far been contemplated, but of Clytemnestra's guilt as part and parcel of the guilts of Atreus and Thyestes, that is, of a chain of obvious crimes, crimes lacking the ambiguity, or mingled right and wrong, of Agamemnon's act at Aulis.

The innocence of Agamemnon, seen in contrast with Clytemnestra's deliberate wickedness and the daimonic Erinys of the house, now emerges. His guilt will be obliterated by his death. Is his death to perpetuate the fatality of his house, to be another crime in a chain of equal crimes, or unique and involving a unique retribution? This does not become clear until the end of the trilogy, but the emergence of Apollo in the Cassandra scene does associate Orestes with the Olympians (and Zeus behind them) in a decisively new way. There is something different about Agamemnon's murder. It is not gratuitous, without moral excuse—Aeschylus went to enormous pains to make this clear, and had to make it clear if his theory of Zeus and *dike* was to stand up—but it lays a vastly greater burden of real guilt upon its perpetrator, so that the justice of *her* retribution can assume a wholly new clarity, and force the Olympians to show their hand.

All this, however, is more of a revelation than a surprise. Up to this point Clytemnestra has dominated the action, has shown her true character and intentions in her increasingly hypocritical speech and behavior, while the chorus has veiled all this in language of both designed obscurity and actual ignorance. It has been concerned with the "guilt" of Agamemnon as the vaguely envisaged cause of a downfall that would somehow obliterate his victorious return. It has seen Clytemnestra as an evil adulteress, as a wronged mother, but not as a prospective murderess; it has, like Agamemnon, discounted her resources of energy and will power. This was underneath its emphatic "silence" on the matter. The truth comes out—though even now in a way that the chorus cannot finally grasp, for Cassandra is still the frustrated prophetess—and we see that Clytemnestra is the crucial figure, her guilt the important guilt of the trilogy, her fate the decisive test of Zeus' *dike*. Agamemnon is transformed: once dead or counted as dead, it is his royalty, his righteousness and heroism, that come to the fore. The disparity of guilts that alone can justify Orestes' matricide is at last established.

The awful pause that the whole Cassandra episode represents is brought out by the dramatic device of her silence—the moments when she sits alone in the car and seems to take no heed of the expostulations of Clytemnestra and the well meant advice of the chorus. Agamemnon has gone in. Clytemnestra is anxious to get her other victim in also. She will not force the issue or waste words; Cassandra is not in a position to hold out. Whether or not we are meant to infer that her delayed entrance was to be the signal of the double murder—the exact moment that Clytemnestra had in mind—we know that Cassandra is a true prophetess who will take the right time for her entrance. For a moment the clock has stopped.

The fate of Cassandra is forecast by Clytemnestra's hypocritical double meanings in much the same manner as that of Agamemnon. The sacrificial animals, Clytemnestra declares, are waiting for the slaughter. Cassandra must attend the ceremony with the other slaves, but she has not yet learned to bear the bridle without a bloody resistance. This renewed demonstration of Clytemnestra's macabre hypocrisy sets the key of the kommos, and shows the relation of the murderess to her innocent victim.

Cassandra's first utterances are brief, enigmatic invocations of Apollo. Her appeal marks the introduction of a major motif:

Apollo himself. The murders become his direct concern from the moment of his invocation here. But the Aeschylean play on words is striking; his name also implies death and destruction: Ἄπολλον· Ἄπολλον· / ἀγυιᾶτ', ἀπόλλων ἐμός (1080–81; 1085–86). The initial contrast of the chorus's prosaic trimeters with Cassandra's lyric bacchiacs, iambs, and dochmiacs is effective; the voice of anguished prophecy contends against an uncomprehending literalism. The impending murder and the terrible crime of Atreus (the cannibal banquet) come out in brief lyric vignettes until at last the chorus itself is moved to lyric utterance: despite its distrust of ominous prophecy, it is forced under Cassandra's influence to reiterate its sense of impending doom. The cannibal banquet is an old story, but the other things—the blood on the house, the great evil impending there, the wife washing the husband in the bath, the hand that stretches and stretches again, the terrible snare and net, the inscrutable Stasis or Erinys, the bull and the cow and the cauldron—are all beyond the chorus's grasp. The chorus understands that Cassandra is predicting her own doom and it comprehends her references to the destruction of Troy, but it sees only a general malignity or vague *daimon* at work.

The emotional intensity and dramatic power of this part of the kommos have often been noted. Cassandra's words are tragic in themselves, but particularly so next to the uncomprehending ignorance of the chorus. She is trying to break loose from her condition—her imposed inability to be understood—under an almost unbearable stress of emotion. It is her emotion that as yet disturbs the clarity of her vision.

The shift at 1178 from lyric to iambic trimeter and from disjointed allusion to sequential statement marks a tremendous effort at self-control, a final determination to induce understanding. This is the moment of revelation, the moment that sets Agamemnon's fate in the context of his house and its history, the elemental spirits at work there, the avenger to come, and the gods behind him. Agamemnon's murder is set in a context which relates it to the past and insists on its determination of the future.

The emphasis shifts from his guilt to his wife's and his ancestors' and thus to that of his house and the Erinyes in his house. Three speeches deal with each stage of the problem: the first (1178–97) with the origin of the fatal Erinyes, their loathing for the adultery of Thyestes, the crime done to Atreus; the second (1214–41) with the vengeance of Atreus on Thyestes (the cannibal banquet) and the consequent vengeance for it plotted by Aegisthus and Clytemnestra; the third (1256–95) with her own death and the avenger who will come, led by the gods, to do herself and Agamemnon justice. The first speech describes the Erinyes of the house and traces their origin to the initial crime, the infatuation (πρώταρχον ἄτης, 1192)—i.e., the adultery—of Thyestes. The important point is that they have come to stay, or are very difficult to dispel (κῶμος ἐν δόμοις μένει, / δύσπεμπτος ἔξω, 1189–90):

> τὴν γὰρ στέγην τήνδ' οὔποτ' ἐκλείπει χορὸς
> σύμφθογγος οὐκ εὔφωνος· οὐ γὰρ εὖ λέγει.
> καὶ μὴν πεπωκώς γ', ὡς θρασύνεσθαι πλέον   (1186–88)

What is particularly notable is the completely amoral or indeed immoral character of the Erinyes. They are not divinities of "just" vengeance; they are concerned with vengeance *per se* and observe no proportion between the original deed and the deed that avenges it. They loathe the defilement of Atreus' bed, but they encourage a vengeance much more horrible than the defilement itself. Man is here subject to a frightful, inhuman, and unjust necessity that is not offset by his own concomitant guilt.

Cassandra's second speech connects the adultery of Thyestes with the vengeance of Atreus—the cannibal feast. A rather emotional reference suffices for this; it is well known to the chorus, as it is far in the past. The next vengeance (the murder of Agamemnon) is determined by the crime of Atreus and involves primarily Aegisthus—the son and proper avenger of Thyestes—with whom Clytemnestra is associated as a wanton paramour and adultress. Aegisthus is the "craven lion in the bed" (λέοντ' ἄναλκιν, ἐν λέχει στρωφώμενον, 1224), i.e., Agamemnon's bed. Clytemnestra's hypocritical words to Agamemnon are seen as shameless. Cassandra does not mention Iphigenia. No crime is attributed to Agamemnon: he is the "commander of the ships and overthrower of Ilium" wantonly attacked by the "hateful bitch," the "treacherous" ἄτη (1230), the "female slayer of the male," an amphisbaena or snake-like Scylla, a raging mother of Hell, trucelessly at war with her kin. The premise of Cassandra is that there was no motive for the crime but Aegisthus' desire to avenge the deed of Atreus on his innocent son, and Clytemnestra's desire to aid and abet her paramour. Clytemnestra, "the two-footed lioness," lies with the "wolf" (to whom Aegisthus is also likened) in the absence of Agamemnon, "the noble lion" (λέοντος εὐγενοῦς ἀπουσίᾳ, 1259).

Cassandra's animus may be directed against Clytemnestra because Clytemnestra will be her own murderess. There seems, nonetheless, to be much more than that in Aeschylus' language. He is concerned to pass over the guilt of Agamemnon. The vengeance of Orestes, which Cassandra prophesies in her third speech, is represented as just and is attributed to the gods themselves. And "gods" here (ἐκ θεῶν, 1280) can only mean the Olympians, not the Erinyes of the house. This is evident from her previous insistence on Apollo as the one who led her to death, the one who now strips her of her prophetic insignia (1265). Apollo and the gods associated with him will see that she is avenged. Her final prayer for vengeance is addressed to the Sun (who is also Apollo). The Erinyes of the house would not be interested in avenging her, yet she speaks of Orestes as "our" avenger (ἡμῶν . . . τιμάορος, 1280), i.e., the avenger of *both* Cassandra and Agamemnon. In short, the entire emphasis here is on the guilt of Clytemnestra: Orestes is called "mother-slayer" (μητροκτόνον, 1281), precisely because Clytemnestra as adulteress, murderess, and "unnatural" monstrosity is the real culprit.

Aegisthus is also to blame, but vengeance on him is never considered problematic or questionable: that he did not take a direct part in the murder is proof only of his cowardice as opposed to the effrontery of his "male-like" paramour. Sophocles, who obviously wanted to write a relatively simple vengeance drama, reversed the emphasis and made the killing of Aegisthus the climax and conclusion of his play.

The previous insistence on Agamemnon's guilt is not canceled. Iphigenia has not been forgotten, as Clytemnestra will later make clear. Cassandra leaves in almost total obscurity the future of the Erinyes of the house, who, we have been told, will never leave it or will at any rate be hard to expel. If the Olympian gods are now to take vengeance or to see to it that Orestes acts as their representative, we can only wonder where this leaves the Erinyes and what it does to their role as the avenging power in the house of Atreus. Aeschylus had only two choices. He could (as he did in the *Septem contra Thebas*) represent the Erinyes as cooperating with Apollo and the Olympians, so that the latter only would be concerned with the avenging of Agamemnon. But it is hard to see how he could have made them cooperate with the Olympians after he had so clearly emphasized—particularly in the first Cassandra speech—their evil and bloodthirsty character, their specialization in crimes like the cannibal feast and the murder of Agamemnon. Here lies the reason for his limitation of the role of the Erinyes (to violence in the matrilineal line), and their decisive separation from the Olympians. Such a limitation and separation, as Friedrich Solmsen has pointed out,[1] is not at all evident in the earlier literature and not really evident before the *Eumenides*.

This problem does not become at all obtrusive or dominant

1. *Hesiod and Aeschylus* (Ithaca, 1949) 178–214, esp. 181–82, 186–89.

until the moment (in the *Choephoroe*) when Agamemnon is avenged by Orestes' killing of his own mother. Then the Furies emerge because there is no surviving human relative in a position to take on the job of avenging her. The attribution of this vengeance to the Erinyes was part of the tradition, as we can see from Stesichorus' *Oresteia*.[2] Aeschylus had more in mind than this. The murder of Agamemnon raised the whole question of guilt and revenge in relation to the *dike* of Zeus. It made the vengeance of Orestes necessary, even from the Olympian viewpoint, but it could not settle the question of its justice. Orestes could not be left as fully justified τιμάορος (1280), henceforth immune from the vengeance that ran in his house. The paradigmatic or theological point of the tragedy would be reduced to almost nothing. The crisis that forced Orestes to kill his mother and the gods to urge him to do so would have had no explanation. The murder of Agamemnon would also have lacked any meaning: it might be avenged in a human sense, but the supernatural forces behind it would have been involved in a quite unendurable ambiguity of guilt. Was it Zeus or the Erinyes that led Agamemnon to his death? What was the role of his human guilt or responsibility? Was there no line at all to be drawn between the highly disparate agencies at work? Was *dike* to remain in such agonized obscurity? The old code of vengeance was itself the cause of the successive chain of crimes. Olympian necessity as well as human impulse could urge Orestes on as Agamemnon had been driven, but other, fiercer, and less moral forces—the terrible Erinyes—were also at work. Not until they had been clearly differentiated and assimilated to Zeus' overruling justice could the central problem be solved.

The emergence of the Erinyes in the Cassandra kommos begins the polarization of forces that alone can lead to their eventual harmony. The old dispensation, as set forth by the chorus in the parodos and stasima, was viewed almost exclusively from the standpoint of Zeus and the Olympians. Artemis had imposed the necessity under which Agamemnon had so fatally changed. Zeus alone taught wisdom by suffering. Cassandra adds to this picture the terrible demons of the Argive dynasty. Between their vengeance and that now entrusted to Apollo, there seems to be no common ground, no common justice. But the very deepening or expansion of the forces at work in the old dispensation—and now their incipient polarization—reveals the problem of that dispensation and at the same time the necessity of its solution. Orestes will be the figure around whom they must now converge in polarized animosity. On his fate the whole future will depend.

This consideration explains the function of the kommos. The murder of Agamemnon separates the two final kommoi of the play—that between the chorus and Cassandra and that between the chorus and Clytemnestra—and places his own fate in the perspective of the future, of the impending new dispensation. To Clytemnestra, as Cassandra foretells, the Erinys of the Argive house is at work; by her and it the chain of Argive crimes is carried. Apollo is the destined avenger of Agamemnon or punisher of Clytemnestra. We are prepared by Cassandra for the murder and its consequences. It is not until the chorus can confront the fact and its terrible authoress that they can grasp the point of Cassandra's revelation. Then they are at last able to put together the two aspects of the old dispensation—the Olympian or Zeus-*dike* aspect stressed in the parodos and stasima and the retributory or Erinys aspect stressed by Cassandra—and so realize the problem of *dike* in a new way. The two great kommoi, one prophetic, the other retrospective and directly contemplating the awful future ahead, carry us beyond the relatively static world of parodos and stasima into an emergent world of entirely new problems and possibilities. A great change has taken place.

After Cassandra goes into the palace—to her death—the chorus utters a few anapaestic lines (1331–42) of reflection on the increasingly ominous situation of Agamemnon. It does not understand the prophecies of Cassandra, but its premonition of Agamemnon's doom is reinforced. It connects this, as it did not before, with the evil that runs in his house, the house of Atreus. It had already seen that evil prosperity has a habit of begetting disaster (third stanza) and had vaguely suggested a parallel between Paris and Agamemnon; now it explicitly states that no man ever bars the door to prosperity—saying to it "Enter no more"—and so implies that no one can escape the doom of excess prosperity. Here is Agamemnon, the conqueror of Troy, the divinely honored man: if he should pay for the blood spilled by those before him (νῦν δ᾽ εἰ προτέρων αἷμ᾽ ἀποτείσει, 1338) and by his own death atone for their deaths, who could ever after hope for immunity? The ambiguity is thicker than ever. The chorus had up to this point thought mainly in terms of Zeus and his *dike* and of suffering as Zeus's lesson to man. It had rejected the simple and amoral view that prosperity of itself brought retribution. Now it is impressed by Cassandra's insistence on the successive woes of the house of Atreus. If Agamemnon is to be involved in them, to pay somehow for the blood or the crimes of his house, how can there be any security or any justice left? All its meditations have left it hopeless before a great dilemma, and one in which the anticipated woe seems to have eclipsed all hopes of a just prosperity.

At this point, the old men hear the terrible cries of Agamemnon from the palace. Their feeble helplessness is evident in their confused attempt to meet the situation. The last one to speak avers that the best thing is to know "clearly" (τρανῶς, 1371) what has happened to Agamemnon, whereat the doors open and Clytemnestra is seen standing beside the bodies, Agamemnon's lying naked in the bathtub caught in the meshes of a rich and very bloody piece of tapestry. The scene is meant to shock. This disgraceful, ignominious exposure of the trapped victim gives the crime a horror that surpasses that of an ordinary murder. The hypocritical Clytemnestra now, for the first time, shows her true nature in a hideous display of shameless exultation. Her first words reveal the change:

> πολλῶν πάροιθεν καιρίως εἰρημένων
> τἀναντί᾽ εἰπεῖν οὐκ ἐπαισχυνθήσομαι.   (1372–73)

She exposes everything and stands in the very place where she struck the blow—so that all can savor the sweetness of her revenge. She shows how she put him in a position of utter helplessness:

> οὕτω δ᾽ ἔπραξα—καὶ τάδ᾽ οὐκ ἀρνήσομαι—
> ὡς μήτε φεύγειν μήτ᾽ ἀμύνεσθαι μόρον.   (1380–81)

She shows the terrible net. Two blows under the circumstances were enough to dispatch him, but she added a third by way of prayer to Zeus and received in the shower of his arterial blood a drenching as welcome to her as dew to the growing grain. She bids the chorus rejoice if they can. As for herself, she rejoices and glories in the deed and would, if possible, pour a libation on the corpse.

The scene is climactic not simply because of its spectacular horror—the shocking indignity of Agamemnon's position—but because of Clytemnestra's blatant dropping of the hypocritical mask. The secret, ominous obscurity of her prior activity is replaced by an equally deceitful publicity. The murky forebodings of the chorus, which even the prophecies of Cassandra had not been able to clarify, are suddenly realized. The contrast between the doubtful guilt of Agamemnon and the blatant, evident guilt of Clytemnestra is now seen to have underlain the whole drama, but the difference between suspicion and realization is immense. The problem of Agamemnon's guilt is relegated to the dead past, or rather becomes the problem of Clytemnestra's guilt, and the guilt of the whole house of Atreus. Everything that has been ominously festering in the dark now bursts, like a punctured ulcer, into bloody actuality.

The chorus must confront reality, the reality represented by the unmasked and uninhibited Clytemnestra. The revelation of the murder has changed the character of the play. The morality of the parodos and the stasima—its ambiguity, its conception of human guilt and the teaching of Zeus—is set in a different light and is transformed. This is what the murder and its brutal revelation have been designed to effect. Though in one sense interpreted by Cassandra's prophecies, it has also been obscured by them, for Cassandra was doomed to be misunderstood. Cassandra's words have now, and only now, their full effect. The Erinys she had declared to be at work, the human snake through which it worked, have now cast off their disguises and brutally proclaimed themselves. New questions can now emerge. What indeed has been learned by all this suffering? What have been the roles of the fatal Erinys, of Zeus, of Clytemnestra herself? Where lies the guilt and how can the bloodshed be stopped? Even the vengeance of Orestes which Cassandra had predicted does not seem a solution. The dialogue (kommos and epirrhema) between Clytemnestra and the chorus marks a quite new stage in the play and the trilogy.

The chorus is overwhelmed, but it recognizes that such wickedness has to be punished. Clytemnestra must be cast out, banished from the city. But Clytemnestra cares nothing for such threats; she will yield only to superior might. The weak should show discretion (τὸ σωφρονεῖν, 1425, which under the circumstances is a terrible word to use). But the chorus now demands a proper punishment, a punishment of blow for blow (τύμμα τύμματι τεῖσαι, 1430).

Clytemnestra has her answer ready (1431–47). Hers is an act of *dike*, consummated in behalf of her dead child (μὰ τὴν τέλειον τῆς ἐμῆς παιδὸς δίκην, 1432). She has no fear of consequences while Aegisthus shares her hearth. Agamemnon and his concubine— their association is, in her eyes, one of wanton sexuality—have gotten their deserts. Cassandra was the final "tidbit" (παροψώνημα, 1447) to garnish the luxury (χλιδῇ, 1447) of her revenge. The chorus changes (1448) to express pity and grief for its fallen *phylax*, its well-meant protector and king. Dead at a woman's hands! The thought turns its mind back to that symbol of feminine wickedness, Helen. She was indeed an Eris (1461), a demon of strife in the house! But there is no point, as Clytemnestra reminds them, in blaming Helen as if she alone had destroyed all those men.

Not Helen, but the Atridae, should be blamed. Yet the chorus sees Helen and Clytemnestra alike as the loathsome agents of the *daimon* of the house, a *daimon* that works through women and is now singing its tuneless hymn over the corpse.

At this point (1475), Clytemnestra's language and attitude seem to change: in blaming the *daimon* of the race (δαίμονα γέννης, 1477) the chorus has at last hit on the truth. It is the *daimon*—now gorged with the blood of three victims (Thyestes, Iphigenia, and Agamemnon)—who has done it. He has put the love of blood (ἔρως αἱματολοιχός, 1478) in human stomachs and added new gore (νέος ἰχώρ, 1480) to the still festering gore of the past. Clytemnestra now sees her own crime as a quasi-objective thing, a part of the fatality of the house for which she is not personally responsible. She is no longer the grim murderess but an agent of a fatal and dreadful demon.

The chorus understands the terrible ambiguity of the explanation (1481–82). Yes, the demon she mentions is indeed terrible and evil, an insatiable destroyer of the house. But it is not the demon alone that has been at work: Zeus is still the cause and the doer of everything (διαὶ Διὸς / παναιτίου πανεργέτα, 1485–86). What happens among men that is not ordained by Zeus? Here the two supernatural powers (the Erinys or *daimon*; Zeus) are placed in conjunction. The real problem of the trilogy begins to emerge. The chorus sees that its own reflections on Agamemnon's guilt and Zeus' justice must be squared with the bloodthirsty Erinys to which Cassandra had attributed the evil destiny of the house. The ambiguity has begun to break, or at least to reveal the contradictions that had so far been obscured.

Now (1496) Clytemnestra insists on the question of her responsibility. The chorus should not think that the deed is hers (αὐχεῖς εἶναι τόδε τοὔργον ἐμόν, 1497). The old cruel avenger of Thyestes, the Erinys of the house, has taken on her shape (φανταζόμενος δὲ γυναικί, 1500) and made Agamemnon pay for his crime to Iphigenia (τόνδ' ἀπέτεισεν, / τέλεον νεαροῖς ἐπιθύσας, 1503–4).

The chorus is faced with the question of human responsibility. To the problem of the relation of Zeus' will to that of the household Erinys is added the problem of the human will involved. The chorus's answer is to assert her guilt—her human responsibility—but acknowledge the shared guilt of the Erinys. She cannot be guiltless, ἀναίτιος (1505); that in the light of what they have just seen would be abhorrent. Yet an avenging spirit, an avenger of the house of Atreus' crime, might well be present also (πατρόθεν δὲ / συλλήπτωρ γένοιτ' ἂν ἀλάστωρ, 1507–8). There is an Ares in the picture, a demon ever wading through fresh streams of blood, a frost that eats the young of each new generation. The chorus's reflections are followed by a repeated lament for the murdered man, and an insistence on the foulness of the deed and its female author. Yet Clytemnestra will not admit the "ignobility" (οὔτ' ἀνελεύθερον, 1521) of the deed. Agamemnon has suffered in fair requital for his sacrifice of Iphigenia. He has paid for what he did (ξιφοδηλήτῳ / θανάτῳ τείσας ἄπερ ἔρξεν, 1528–29).

The chorus does not know what to think (1530–31). It characterizes the Erinys (Moira) as a continual sharpener of whetstones for the doing of new crimes in the interest of *dike*. The shower of blood will never cease.

The final exchange of words between it and Clytemnestra (1538–76) starts with the question of Agamemnon's burial. How can Clytemnestra dare to bury or bewail the husband she has murdered? Clytemnestra has no intention of bewailing him, though she insists on her right to bury him. Let the dead Iphigenia meet and kiss him when he reaches the Styx! At this point, the chorus perceives the folly of matching taunt with taunt; the matter is hard to decide (δύσμαχα δ' ἐστὶ κρῖναι, 1561). Crime seems to follow crime, or vengeance vengeance: φέρει φέροντ', ἐκτίνει δ' ὁ καίνων (1562). So long as Zeus sits on his throne, the doer will suffer (π α θ ε ῖ ν   τ ὸ ν   ἔ ρ ξ α ν τ α, 1564). That is the rule (θέσμιον γάρ, 1564). How then can the curse be expelled from the house? The whole race of Atreus is "glued" to ruin (ἄτᾳ, 1566). In this pronouncement of "oracle" (χρησμός, 1568), Clytemnestra agrees, but sees a possible remedy. She is now willing to swear an oath to the *daimon* of the house that she will accept the situation and forego further bloodshed if he will leave the house and attach himself to some other family. She wants to rid her halls of all this reciprocal murdering (ἀλληλοφόνους, 1576). Here the argument ends.

In this kommos between Clytemnestra and the chorus, an originally brutal confrontation—the exultant murderess facing the shocked elders—has become a much more ambivalent exchange of views on a common problem: the presence of the *daimon* or Erinys of the house. The chorus sees that there are at least three factors—Clytemnestra, the Erinys, and Zeus—each of whom has some responsibility for what has happened. The doer must pay—here the Erinys and Zeus are in agreement—but this principle holds little hope for the house. Clytemnestra sees her own deed as a final act that may serve to expel the *daimon*; she is not, like the chorus, concerned with Zeus and his overriding will. She has tried to reach some accommodation with the chorus: her attitude has changed. She too has been motivated by her own *dike*, her desire to avenge

Iphigenia, and once this is satisfied, she has ceased to be the hypocritical, brutal man-woman of the murder and the preliminary episodes.

The murder has emerged as a problem in itself: if, as the chorus suggests, the perpetrator or doer must pay, how can the chain of vengeances ever stop? That Clytemnestra can actually make a compact with the horrible Erinys seems wishful thinking; the guilty person cannot control or abolish his own punishment. Nevertheless, her purpose is a good one. It recognizes the necessity of ridding the house of the *daimon* to which, as the chorus has agonizingly cried, it seems permanently glued. The murder has raised more problems than it solved, but the very raising of them is an indispensable condition of their solution. The deed of Clytemnestra is not devoid of *dike*, horrible as it is. She is not simply wicked, without any excuse. The matter is more complicated than one of simple revenge. Even more important, the roles of Zeus and the Erinys have begun to distinguish themselves. There is a certain justice in both, but the latter is motivated by something more primitive than justice: by a love of blood and death. Yet if the Olympians are to insist upon the punishment of Clytemnestra, they must come to terms with this primitive force, or distinguish *their* vengeance from *its*.

The chain of vengeance must be broken. Otherwise there will be no peace or justice left. This kommos suggests the impossibility of breaking it by any further act of bloodshed. Agamemnon's *relative* innocence demanded another act of vengeance; but it was up to Zeus, not the Erinys, to see to it that this vengeance was final. All the Erinys wants is more blood. The remarkable thing about this curious kommos—this strange aftermath of the murder—is the way in which it so quickly disposes of the murder's finality. The difference from a Sophoclean dénouement is marked. It is not the fact of the murder but its effect on the future that matters. We see this in a different way from that of the Cassandra episode. There everything was involved in the tension of the expected event. The future, though prophesied, was not yet present. Cassandra thought only in terms of the terrible *daimon*, the chain of crimes, her anticipated revenge, and the impending murders (including her own). Here the argument has already begun to go beyond revenge, in a way that to discount the murder of Clytemnestra herself. But the obscurity still prevails and a new tension has already begun to build up.

The final scene (1577–1673) brings on Aegisthus (the belatedness of his entrance is significant) and reestablishes the peculiar ambivalence of Clytemnestra's character. Here is the man whose vengeance (for his father Thyestes) she had taken into her own hands—but this Clytemnestra is only part of Aegisthus' boastful fantasy. He claims to be Agamemnon's slayer despite his absence from the scene and despite the fact that he is speaking for himself, not Clytemnestra. Her real motive, as we have long known, is hardly that of avenging Thyestes. The insolence and brashness of Aegisthus finds no response from Clytemnestra. She stops his threats against the chorus and reiterates her desire to avoid further bloodshed. There has already been enough suffering: πημονῆς δ' ἅλις γ' ὑπάρχει· μηδὲν αἱματώμεθα (1656).

Yet she also asserts both his authority and her own: ⟨ἐγὼ⟩ / καὶ σὺ θήσομεν κρατοῦντε τῶνδε δωμάτων ⟨καλῶς⟩ (1672–73). The chorus that threatens her is dependent upon her protection, her influence on Aegisthus. An intolerable situation exists: the criminals are left in possession of the fruits of their crime. Agamemnon's murder cries for the vengeance that the chorus suggests at the end by its reference to Orestes' return (1646). But the scene is not without a hint of further ambiguity. Clytemnestra is not an Aegisthus. In both her superior courage and her greater sensitivity to the consequences of her deed, the need for some sort of peace, she is more than a villainess, at once unwomanly and wanton. She must pay for her crime and die, but her murder will not be an unambiguous act of vengeance without further consequences. Aeschylus makes a clear distinction between Aegisthus, the cowardly adulterer and intriguer, the bad man, and the enigmatic Clytemnestra, whose motives and character are more complex. When Agamemnon disregarded her feelings as mother—the mother of Iphigenia—he gave a fatal twist to her whole character. And it is as a mother that she will confront Orestes. The emphasis and nature of the *Choephoroe* are distinctly, if faintly, foreshadowed.

We can now see why the *Agamemnon* is so much longer than the other plays of the trilogy. It is the long choral passages and the two kommoi and epirrhemata that give salience and meaning to the bare events—the return and the murder—and do so in a dramatic rather than a static or expository way. Agamemnon's return is invested with a dreadful ambiguity, as is the whole expedition from which he returns. It is just and divinely sanctioned (by Zeus) and at the same time enveloped in guilt and the aura of retribution. Agamemnon himself is both righteous and guilty. The guilt is attached to the sacrifice of Iphigenia or, more precisely, to what the necessity of the sacrifice did to his character. There is a vague, yet deeply felt, connection between Agamemnon and the obvious culprits, Paris and Helen. The attitude of the gods comes out in

the circumstances of his return: while the other Greeks are punished by a sea storm, a god takes over the tiller of Agamemnon's
ship and guides it to safety. He is saved for a more horrible penalty.
The herald episode, like the watchman episode, puts the words of
the chorus into terms of actual events and gives them dramatic
setting and meaning. The plot against Agamemnon—the doings
in Argos, the relations of Aegisthus and Clytemnestra—is evil,
as the dark hints of the watchman and the chorus suggest.

Aside from the Olympians and the *dike* of Zeus that bulk so
large in the first three episodes and stasima, there is a different evil
closer to home. This emerges in the Cassandra scene, where we
see the approaching end of Agamemnon in the context of a frightful succession of domestic crimes, represented as the joint act of a
mad, bloodthirsty, insatiable demon or Erinys and that monstrous
snake, the unfeminine woman Clytemnestra. What, then, is the
connection between Zeus, who teaches wisdom by suffering, who
insists that the doer of a crime pay the penalty, and the Fury who
wants more blood? What do the respective guilts of Agamemnon
and Clytemnestra have to do with each other? We are certain that
Agamemnon is less "guilty" or more "innocent" than his hypocritical and blatant murderess, even if we do not see what difference this makes. But the problem has now devolved on Orestes
together with the Olympians and cannot stop short of its solution.
The murder of Agamemnon has broken through a thick cloud of
past ambiguity and guilt to set in train a new succession of different
and healing events—in human terms, a new kind of *dike*; in divine
terms, a new sort of theodicy. That is what the chorus has cried
for, what even Clytemnestra has hinted at, what the ignominious
suffering of Agamemnon most of all seems to demand.

The play is not fully comprehensible in terms of its bare ideas.
It is first of all a poem. And it is a poem that is also a drama. It
is of particular importance to see the dramatic impact of its poetical images or motifs, for such devices as motif-inversion, motif-
fluidity, and motif-transformation (all very much the same in net
effect), are essentially dramatic. Ordinary phenomena which normally are joyous or healthy, are inverted, or made to change sides
and given an unusual fluidity that reveals a cosmic confusion,
something like the "fair is foul and foul is fair" of *Macbeth*. Clytemnestra's hypocritically perverted use of bright colors and sounds,
and strange delight in the perversion of natural scenery—most
notably when she compares the dew on the growing crops with
Agamemnon's arterial blood—are illustrations of a common Aeschylean technique that we find throughout the play. Consider,
for example, the herald's account of the corpses that "blossom" in

the sea. Winds or breezes, to take another instance, are horribly ambivalent: their absence at Aulis is ruinous; their presence on the Aegean is suddenly destructive; they are rich with the aroma of ruin at Troy. What is ostensibly luxurious (like the purple tapestries) is actually baleful (we never forget that purple is the color of blood).[3] Brilliant colors and shrill sounds are almost always inverted so as to suggest the opposite of normal joy.

The play abounds in special images that are repeated and inverted in different contexts and fluidly pass from one side to the other. The net and yoke, eagle and vulture, hare, lion, and snake motifs are symbols, but their subtle intermixture and combination with shifting rhythms and moods and in shifting contexts is anything but obvious. Their recurrence in both lyric and iambic trimeter passages is particularly effective. We have referred to Clytemnestra's choice of revealing metaphor (e.g., the net in her speech of welcome to Agamemnon) and the different use of metaphors in lyric and iambic trimeter portions of the Cassandra scene. These inversions are all affected by the dramatic movement of the play. Perhaps the most important (and most neglected) feature of the *Agamemnon* is the dramatic expression of motif by sound-sense correspondence. The location and collocation of words in different metrical frames is particularly significant. The Aeschylean intention is evident from his obvious punning on such names as Helen and Apollo. This is the superficial aspect of a much broader and deeper phenomenon, the association of specific sounds and rhythms with specific motifs. A number of "sound" words, for example, have a dramatic-liturgical significance (for sound is action; this is why Iphigenia must be gagged at her sacrifice: any expression of pain would undermine the efficacy of the ceremony). The hypocritical victory shrieks of Clytemnestra, the clear voice of Iphigenia at her father's banquet (as well as her later gagging), the first exclamation of Cassandra, the triumphant shout of the watchman, the last cries of the dying Agamemnon, are all interrelated in a fluid interchange of weal and woe. Aeschylus' decided preference of metaphor to simile, his occasional straining of grammar and ordinary usage, are demanded by what we may call his "motif strategy"—his fluid handling of meanings and contexts, words and sounds.

What determines Aeschylus' use of language, metaphor, and motif is their correlation with dramatic shifts of context. Both episode and stasimon not only oppose different elements—basically

3. Robert F. Goheen, "Aspects of Dramatic Symbolism: Three Studies in the *Oresteia*," *American Journal of Philology* 76 (1955) 113–37, esp. 115–16.

good and bad—but transform them into one another as the action progresses. As the point of view shifts, the language shifts with it. This is evident in Aeschylus' use of characterization. The watchman, the chorus, Clytemnestra, the herald, Agamemnon, Cassandra, and Aegisthus each reveal a distinctive approach or way of feeling and thinking. The watchman is not a complex or hypocritical personality; his enforced silence, the necessity of repressing his feelings, comes hard. The chorus is not simply a mouthpiece of the poet but a real voice of the confused, pious, anxious, war-wearied but still loyal elder citizenry of Argos. Clytemnestra is ominously hypocritical, then brutally frank, with depths of feeling and reflection behind both moods. She is a woman with manlike force, a manlike capacity to serve her own ends, yet with a maternal motivation behind them. The basis of her attachment to Aegisthus is not clear, but though she is to Cassandra and the chorus an evil and wanton woman, she is not so represented in the closing scene, where from beneath her hypocrisy and brutality an anxiety, a sense of the very evil she represents, begins to emerge. The herald is aware of his duty to give good news when his news in fact is mixed—this is the herald stereotype—but he is also the voice of the army, of the soldiers glad to be back, conscious of physical inconvenience finally surmounted. Agamemnon is arrogant, insensitive, conventional, hardened, unaware of other people's real feelings. Cassandra, the captive, degraded prophetess, bearer of a doom she cannot tell, caught in the snare of her own sexual attractiveness, is a complete foil to the grim Clytemnestra. Aegisthus, the "cowardly lion," is all brag and bluster with little force or initiative. Each of these characters gives a different slant to the dominant motifs of the poem, much as do the different meters of the lyrics. How differently the fatal net is treated by Cassandra, Clytemnestra, and the chorus; the taking of Troy, by Clytemnestra, Agamemnon, the herald, and the chorus; the Thyestean banquet, by Cassandra and Aegisthus; the beacons, by the watchman, Clytemnestra, and the chorus! Each character has a distinct "theology" or view of the gods; the difference in this respect between the chorus, Clytemnestra, Agamemnon, and Cassandra is especially marked.

The point of importance is what the characterization means to the main movement of ideas and motifs. It is a commonplace criticism that Aeschylus is not so concerned with character as Sophocles.[4] The truth of this is not so clear as some have sup-

---

4. See R. D. Dawe, "Inconsistencies of Plot and Character in Aeschylus," *Proceedings of the Cambridge Philological Society* 189 (1963) 21–62; P. E. Easter-

posed. Aeschylus uses characterization in an un-Sophoclean way. He is not concerned with the fate of an individual, not, e.g., with explaining the tragedy of Agamemnon in terms of his character. Agamemnon's appearance on the stage is brief; he has no opportunity to reveal his personality in any detail. The contrast with Sophocles' Oedipus, who is continuously on stage in *Oedipus Rex*, is great. Agamemnon is doomed; even his guilt is secondary to the more general guilt in which he is involved. This does not mean that his personal guilt is not essential to the drama. It means that his guilt is not degraded to an "Aristotelian" or "Aristotelian-Sophoclean" error, or *hamartia*, or subordinated to characterization conceived as the gradual building up of empathy for the doomed man and of the pity and fear we are supposed to feel for him. Character is important because it is an essential concomitant of will, of intent, of innocence or guilt—of morality, in a word; it is only part of a greater complex. Men are constrained by several kinds of necessity and by the all-reaching justice of Zeus. Agamemnon is presented to us within this context: his is the test case, the case that clarifies. What matters is not what Agamemnon does or suffers but what his action and suffering represent.

From this perspective, we can more easily explain characterization in Aeschylus. We can see why Agamemnon appears only in one brief episode while Clytemnestra appears in all the first three episodes and dominates the final kommos with the chorus. We can see why the other characters—the chorus, the watchman, the herald, Cassandra, and Aegisthus—are each confined to single scenes or episodes, in a particular order of appearance. The chorus is concerned with Agamemnon, with his guilt, with his role as a just and Zeus-sent avenger of Trojan crime, with his ambiguous relation to both the good and bad sides of the war. The watchman and the herald bring out special aspects of the same general problem—the ambiguous mixture of weal and woe, justice and guilt—and give a dramatic present context to the recollective meditation of the chorus, its panoramic recall of the past. Cassandra, the frustrated prophetess, brings out at the proper time the other, the domestic past—the demon of the house—and relates it to present and future, the impending murder and its aftermath. Clytemnestra is a present evil; she is the visible, plotting, tangible agent of the *daimon*, or rather a living blend of personal and collective guilt; she dominates and is meant to dominate the play. It is her character that is most elaborately developed. Up to

ling, "Presentation of Character in Aeschylus," *Greece and Rome*, ser. 2, 20 (1973) 3–19.

the murder, everything she says is an "act": her hypocritical con-
cealment of her intentions is the index of her activity, her plotting
of Agamemnon's destruction. She lives entirely in the present or
for the future. The other characters respond to her activity by an
emphatic silence or by an enigmatic hint. Not until the moment
of the crime is she lyrically linked with the past, the house of
Atreus, and then only by the prophetic Cassandra in a scene where
Clytemnestra herself is conspicuously absent. Before the murder
Clytemnestra stands outside the lyrical portions of the play; she
acts in the present and does not lyrically react to the past or future.
She is the present of the *Agamemnon*: in the next drama (*Choephoroe*)
her role contracts to a small portion of two short episodes and
corresponds to the role of Agamemnon in the preceding play.

The difference here between Aeschylus and either Sophocles or
Euripides is basically one of time,[5] of the relation of present to
past and future or of present to two cosmic-historical *status quo*s,
one in which everything is shrouded in obscurity and beset by
implicit contradictions and one in which everything is clarified or
begins to be clarified and relieved of its obvious contradictions.
Jacqueline de Romilly has described time in Aeschylus as something beyond the "tragic" time of Sophocles or the "pathetic" time
of Euripides; it is "a master . . . [that] teaches a lesson," a "positive and creative power" that brings punishment and makes men
wiser. This is a true and helpful distinction, but not one that gets
at the root problem of Aeschylean time. There is a distinction between the time of the episodes dominated by Clytemnestra—the
real actor or doer of the play—and the time of the choral parodos
and stasima. Here we have the contrast between a past condition
or *status quo*—the war and its causes, the guilt of Agamemnon—
and an incessant present activity, the hypocritical act of Clytemnestra. The distinction is expressed by the metrical difference
between the lyric meters and the iambic trimeter. This differentiation of times is broken by the peculiar present-past-future time of
Cassandra—the blend of retrospect and prophecy in a distended
present, the unnatural interval when the murder hangs fire and the
action is interrupted—and finally by the murder event itself that,
in the final kommos and epirrhema between the chorus and Clytemnestra, creates another or fourth time, a direct combination or
synthesis of past and future. What is decisive is the impact of the
time of the episodes culminating in the murder—the great or deci-

5. See Jacqueline de Romilly, *Time in Greek Tragedy* (Ithaca, 1968) 59–
85 (Aeschylus; material quoted, 60, 67); 87–111 (Sophocles); 113–41
(Euripides).

sive moment of the play—on the first time, or *status quo*. What teaches is not time in its progressive or unfolding aspect—as de Romilly would seem to think—but the momentary time of action, the action that breaks up the first "extended time" or *status quo* and creates the second "extended time" or *status quo*. When Clytemnestra kills Agamemnon, she shifts all the terms of the drama: an old dispensation is replaced by a new.

The difference from Sophocles or Euripides is very striking. Sophocles is concerned with the tragedy *per se*: his *Oedipus, Antigone,* and *Trachiniae* are designed to lead up to a denouement which is not in any sense a new dispensation.[6] Euripides is concerned, primarily, with developing and extending a pathetic effect, and it is this that determines the timing of his plays.[7] Aeschylus is primarily concerned with neither denouement nor pathos. This is why his "hero," Agamemnon, plays so small a part in the drama and his "villain," Clytemnestra, so large a one, or more exactly why Agamemnon is so largely subsumed in the lyric time of the choruses and kommoi and Clytemnestra is centered in the active time of the episodes. Agamemnon belongs to the old dispensation; Clytemnestra, to the moment that changes it. Once it is changed she reverts to the role of passive victim (in the *Choephoroe*). In Sophocles and Euripides the tragedy or suffering of the hero is *per se* determinative and crucial, while in Aeschylus it is only a means to an end, a device that shifts one dispensation into another. This means that Aeschylus' characters do not "count" in the manner of Sophoclean or Euripidean characters. Their guilt or innocence is important insofar as it affects the dispensation, not in respect to its own tragical or pathetic significance.

It is this difference that accounts for the unique relationship between chorus and episode that distinguishes Aeschylus. Two recent dissertations from Tübingen have made this relationship clearer than before and bear out the conclusions I have reached above. Klaus Aichele has carefully diagrammed the relative length of episode (vis à vis parodoi, exodoi, and stasima) in the three tragedies: his analysis, even though in some vital respects incomplete, brings out clearly the unique standing of the *Oresteia* as compared with the dramas of either Sophocles or Euripides or the other dramas of Aeschylus.[8] The *Agamemnon* is unique in the

6. See de Romilly, *Time*, 88–89.
7. See de Romilly, *Time*, 122.
8. "Die Epeisodien der griechischen Tragödie" (1966); his conclusions are summarized in Walter Jens, ed., *Die Bauformen der griechischen Tragödie* (Munich, 1971) 47–84.

length of its parodos and first two stasima—more accurately in respect to the proportions of parodos, stasimon, and episode: a very long parodos followed by three stasima of decreasing length until the final, or third, stasimon approaches "normal" length. The lengthy and specialized character of its "fourth" episode and exodos is also unique. The shorter *Choephoroe* and *Eumenides* reveal a different arrangement, the former containing a first episode that embraces almost half the play, and the latter containing an exodos of disproportionate length. What dominate and are mainly responsible for the length of these sections—the fourth episode and exodos of the *Agamemnon*, the first episode of the *Choephoroe*, and the exodos of the *Eumenides*—are the kommoi and epirrhemata, or lyric and lyric-trimeter dialogues of chorus and actors (Cassandra, Clytemnestra, Electra, and Orestes, the Furies, and Athena). The centers of emphasis are those in which the action (represented by the actors) impinges on the "extended time" of the chorus and changes it to affect a new or different dispensation. The kommos is the crucial part of each play in the *Oresteia*. It is such by and through the way in which it "grows out" of the stasima and episodes. It is the place where the lyrical and dramatic elements of the drama are joined, where that third time—that past-future time as opposed to the past-present of the stasima and the mere present of the nonlyric episodes—is established.

In the other of the two dissertations, Jürgen Rode has pointed out, in a manner similar to my analysis just above, the peculiar continuity of the parodos and stasima of the *Agamemnon*.[9] The stasima are not "mimetic" like those of satyr-plays, but preserve a definite "distance" of theme and tone from the main action. Yet they are not independent of it, like the stasima of Phrynicus (and some of the later Euripides), nor roughly parallel to it like those of Sophocles, nor a sort of intensification of it like many stasima of Euripides, repeating or dwelling on the content and *pathos* of the preceding episode. They are, rather, special developments or continuations of the episode, even while preserving a lyric distance from it. They avoid the "ring composition" that characterizes the Pindaric odes and, in general, the stasima of the other Greek dramatists. While they depart from one episode and lead into another, they are not identical with either episode, in timing or action sequence, but rather a peculiar sort of "comment" on both.

The ambiguity of the episodes—their constant offsetting of weal by woe, good by bad—is paralleled by the ambiguity of the

9. "Untersuchungen zur Form der Aischyleischen Chorliedes" (1965); conclusions summarized in Jens, ed., *Bauformen*, 85–116.

stasima, in which the guilt of Troy, of Paris and Helen, is merged and partially identified with the guilt of the Atridae, of Agamemnon and the war. We see the same progression from the righteousness of Agamemnon and the wickedness of Troy to the culpability of Agamemnon and the wickedness of war itself.

The parodos and first three stasima of the *Agamemnon* are determined by their relation to the episodes. The prologue sets the time of the action (the fall of Troy as announced by the beacons) and the parodos starts from it, or from the sacrifices lit by Clytemnestra to celebrate the good news. The anapaests, dactyls, trochees, and syncopated iambs of the parodos represent a continuous movement in which the shift of meter corresponds to a shift of mood and content. The expectation of the kings' return on this tenth year of the war suggests their original departure; we revert ten years into the past. This past is a continuous narrative. We see the Atridae as avengers of Paris' original crime; as the fateful eagles of the omen; as the objects, therefore, of Artemis' wrath in Calchas' interpretation of the omen; as fulfillers of his words in the dreadful calm at Aulis and the sacrifice it necessitates; as guilty when Agamemnon at last changes under the yoke that the compulsion puts upon him. The consequences of this guilt are still undefined. We go back, at the end of the parodos, to the ambiguity that surrounds his expected return, an ambiguity that the victory over Troy (not yet fully credited) cannot dissipate.

In the first episode we find this ambiguity reiterated by Clytemnestra (the victory offset by the ominous possibility of sacrilege and divine anger) and the focus of attention directed at the war itself. The first stasimon starts from the defeat of Troy (Paris) and ends with the unpopularity and guilt of the Atridae (who have caused and fought the war). It repeats the movement of the parodos, but now in the more explicit context of victory and foreboding suggested by the preceding episode. The weal-woe contrast is then reinforced by the second episode (the herald) with its dual themes of victory and destructive storm. The chorus takes up the cue: the storm suggests Helen—the ship-destroyer—and this in turn suggests the bane—the lion-pet become the lion of destruction—that has ruined Troy, but the lion is also a symbol of all guilty prosperity, a symbol that shifts more and more toward the triumphant Agamemnon. His entrance and walking of the carpet (third episode) suggest a more explicit and intense sense of woe (third stasimon), though without any real change of content or clear basis for the foreboding expressed.

Up to this point, then, we have been teetering on the moment of Agamemnon's return. The episodes progressively intensify its good and bad aspects, the victory that made it possible, the evil circumstances (portents, storm, anger of the gods) that shadow it with the prospect of woe. The parodos and stasima set it in a past perspective and give it a moral interpretation, which together expand its temporal significance and bring the past into the decisive presentness of the action. We are assured of the supreme power of Zeus, the reality of his justice, his teaching of wisdom by suffering. But we do not see how he works, how he could both command the Trojan War and allow the necessity that weighed down Agamemnon with the burden of guilt and impending nemesis. The shadow of Iphigenia falls across the victory. The past invests the present with its own ambiguity.

We stand, marking time, yet with a dreadful sense that time is running out. Agamemnon has been set in a panorama so inclusive and so huge that his own fate has become representative or exemplary of a whole dispensation, the old dispensation whose last hour is also at hand.

Cassandra (fourth episode) breaks both the presentness of the preceding episodes and the pastness of the choral passages. She alone has access to the future and to a past that had as yet been only hinted at, and she relates them to a common cause that she herself introduces into the drama: the Erinys of the house of Atreus. She connects the future with Apollo, who is the author of both her ruin and her prospective vengeance. She is in only partial engagement with the chorus, to whom all her prophecies are necessarily enigmatic. The imminence of change, a new dramatic tension and time, is unmistakable. The fusion of lyric and iambic trimeter measures (especially in Cassandra's own words) corresponds to the new fusion of action and lyric understanding, the new polarization of the divine powers.

The murder is the turning point. (The Cassandra kommos had prepared it without depriving it of its shock.) After it, the kommos and epirrhema become a direct engagement, a dramatic confrontation of the two characters (the chorus and Clytemnestra) who have stood for the past and the present. The problem of guilt assumes a new aspect; the respective roles of Erinys, Zeus, and the individual human being (Clytemnestra), though still ambiguous, are invested with new problematic intensity. It is now only the future that matters. The necessity of solution is manifest, even to Clytemnestra. Here the progression of lyric and trimeter verses is dramatically progressive, unlike the Cassandra kommos or the preceding parodos and stasima.

Together, however, the two kommoi give the murder a meaning that it could not have had without them. The prophetic expectation of the murder by Cassandra in that moment when the clock is arrested, the terrible event put off by her brief delaying of her entrance into the palace, bridges the gap between past and future, between old and new dispensations, and foreshadows that polarization of the divine forces—Erinyes and Olympians—to which the murder itself and the confrontation of Clytemnestra and chorus give a horrible reality. Now time flows on again, but in a different direction. Nothing is what it was: a new dispensation is in the making.

The appearance of Aegisthus marks a new phase. The closing tetrameters represent the temporary triumph of the guilty. But Aegisthus' vow of vengeance on the chorus is answered by the chorus's own appeal to Orestes. The decisive break with the past has taken place.

The unusual length of the play allows the times to be poised against each other, indicating the transition from the past of the parodos and the stasima to the future of the kommoi and the relation of both to the momentary past of the return and the murder (set forth in the episode). It is an error to read the play in terms only of the parodos or stasima or to ignore their difference from the kommoi. The structure of the whole is adapted to its dramatic meaning, the essential shift of all its elements by the decisive action that transmutes an old into a new dispensation. The play reveals not only a difference of times, but of themes or contents that are brought to engagement by the murder and its brutal proclamation. This duality or disparity of themes does not create an effect of disunity or incoherence, because the sudden emergence of the second or counter-theme is itself a result of the previous dramatic action, a realization of hidden events and feelings that have all along been obscurely felt and have been pregnant in the drama from the very first.

The first theme—that of the parodos and stasima and, ostensibly at least, of the first three episodes—is that of the war and the roles therein of Troy and the Atridae. The guilts of each side (e.g., Paris and Helen against Agamemnon) shade into the other, and the war is doubly evil. Nor is this ambiguity confined to mortals: Zeus himself is at once the punisher of Paris and Troy and the prospective punisher of Agamemnon and the Greeks. His complicity with Artemis is obscure, but it is implied, since his overriding power and justice are proclaimed. Agamemnon is both justified and guilty, but his guilt is tied to his justification; it is his Zeus-authorized status as leader of the Greeks that creates the terrible necessity of his sacrifice of Iphigenia, but the sacrifice is a guilty and sinful act, as the conduct of the war confirms and the omen has predicted. Agamemnon's career is an inscrutable union of divine and human responsibility, of justice and guilt.

The second theme is first expressed by Cassandra, when the murder is inevitable: the guilt of the Atreid house, of Atreus, Thyestes, Clytemnestra, and the terrible Erinys. Here there is almost none of the ambiguity of the first theme—the war theme—for the human principals are represented as deliberately wicked, and the divinity concerned—the Erinys—is one of sheer blood-thirstiness and crime. The relation of this divinity to Apollo, whom Cassandra invokes as her and Agamemnon's avenger, is obscure. Zeus is not mentioned. He reemerges only in the final kommos between the chorus and Clytemnestra, and it is then that we see that there are three main causes of the tragedy of Agamemnon: Zeus himself, the all-responsible, all-powerful god; the Argive Erinys or Erinyes; and Clytemnestra, whom the chorus will not exempt from moral guilt and responsibility.

The second theme has been represented by Clytemnestra, and in a hidden way by her paramour Aegisthus. She is the evil genius of Argos. In her the Erinys has been ominously present. The return of Agamemnon is the event that brings him into her sphere of action and directly connects the two themes; even while the first or Trojan theme is uppermost, there is implicit in it a denouement when the Trojan and Argive elements finally merge. So he comes back from Troy and from the war to the scene of his own household's crime. His death represents the result of more than his own guilt at Aulis and Troy. If Clytemnestra avenges the death of Iphigenia—something that had in the parodos been treated only as part of the war—and carries out the justice of Zeus (about which the chorus has so constantly hinted), she likewise represents the evil, ominous Erinys of the Atreid house and personally expresses a more direct and unambiguous guilt of her own.

The polarization of the forces—human and divine—that determine the rest of the trilogy was thus bound to occur. This could only take place when Agamemnon himself had been killed or sacrificed. His guilt was sufficiently ambiguous to justify both his murder and the subsequent avenging of it. Clytemnestra's guilt was not ambiguous in this sense, even though we can already sense that the Erinys will not discriminate. Agamemnon was involved in the criminal history of Argos as well as in the events at Aulis and Troy, and each represented part of the past, the old dispensation, which only his death could bring to an end. The war and its ominous origin had at least been brought home to Argos, so that the final Argive phase of Agamemnon's destiny could swallow up all that had gone before. In human terms, the guilt of Clytemnestra takes precedence over the guilt of Agamemnon.

The contrast of Trojan and Argive themes—of Agamemnon and Clytemnestra, of Zeus and the Erinys, of war and domestic crime—is throughout associated with that between morally ambiguous and morally clarified action. Agamemnon is the ambiguous figure. He is just and guilty, as are the war he wages and the terrible sacrifice he makes at Aulis. His return is both triumphant and ominous, an unnerving mixture of weal and woe. But his murder is evil, as are its perpetrators. The lack of moral equality between his fate and Iphigenia's, between his act and Clytemnestra's, clarifies the situation. Insofar as Clytemnestra represented a divinity or acted under the impulse of a divinity, that divinity could not be permitted to go on without further check. The past is not adequately explained, but it *is* superseded by a new present and future which are not ambiguous in the old sense. This also has been foreshadowed. The very ambiguity of the past, as the chorus retells it, contains a peculiar urgency, as if somehow it were bound to deliver up its secret. It is directed toward the impending woe, the event of Agamemnon's death. For the play has throughout concentrated on the event, so ominous, so dreaded, yet also so invested with hope, which is to decide the issue—to clarify the dreadful ambiguity. The event is in itself a tragedy, but it is providential, for everything indicates that in it the justice of Zeus is at stake.

IV. THE *CHOEPHOROE*

I t is unnecessary to discuss the *Choephoroe* in the same detail as the *Agamemnon*. The issue that concerns me in this study is the nature of Agamemnon's "tragedy," and I shall discuss the other plays of the trilogy only in their relation to this. The question left open at the end of the *Agamemnon* is not the justice or the fact of Orestes' revenge (Cassandra is a true prophetess), but how it can lead to a settlement of the chain of crimes in his house, a *modus vivendi* between Zeus and the family Erinys, a just punishment of human guilt that could be consistent with human peace. If vengeance—the compensatory killings of Clytemnestra and Aegisthus—could have accomplished all this, there would have been no need for the rest of the trilogy. Aeschylus could have indicated at the end of the *Agamemnon* that Cassandra's prophecy would come true, and settled all the points at issue. The murder of Clytemnestra would have been utterly unproblematic. But the chain of crimes had not yet been broken; only the necessity of a solution had been adumbrated. Agamemnon's death had changed all the old, obscure relations of human guilt and divine justice.

The principal structural feature of the *Choephoroe* is the long first episode and kommos of almost exactly five hundred lines (83–582), or half the play. Albin Lesky rightly raised the question of what would happen to this play if the bulk of this scene—or particularly the kommos (305–475)—were omitted.[1] In his view Orestes here assumes primary responsibility for the deed, becomes himself imbued with the desire for vengeance, or ceases to be a mere agent of Apollo, so that he too, like Agamemnon before him, joins guilt with divine necessity and opens himself to the retribution of the Erinyes. It is not, as Wolfgang Schadewaldt thought, that he simply steels himself for the matricide,[2] but that he actively desires it or personally takes on the "yoke of necessity." Aeschylus—unlike Sophocles—insists on the matricide and makes it the decisive event of the play. What Orestes faces is nothing so simple as vengeance on Aegisthus—that is no problem—but the

1. *Der Kommos der Choephoren*, Akademie der Wissenschaften in Wein, phil.-hist. Klasse, Sitzungsberichte 221, 3 (Vienna and Leipzig, 1943).
2. "Der Kommos in Aischylos' *Choephoren*," *Hermes* 67 (1932) 312–54, reprinted in his *Hellas und Hesperien* (Zurich and Stuttgart, 1960) 106–41.

murder of his own mother. According to Lesky, he himself came actively to desire her death and thus to incur his own burden of guilt. Here we can draw a parallel between him and his father, Agamemnon. The latter was not merely constrained, by divine compulsion, to sacrifice his daughter; he himself cooperated and came to want the sacrifice. This was his personal guilt, for which he will be justly punished. Likewise Orestes was not merely constrained (by Apollo's edict) to kill his mother.

The truth, I think, lies between Lesky and Schadewaldt. Lesky is misled by his refusal to make clear distinctions between the different crimes of the house of Atreus. Orestes is commanded by Apollo to commit matricide under the threat of terrible penalties if he refuses. Furthermore, the matricide is justified by the sheer wickedness of his mother. She cannot be left unpunished. She is no innocent like Iphigenia. She is also different from her victim, Agamemnon. No external necessity, no terrible, ineluctable choice (a choice between divine wills as well as between human duties and feelings) constrained her to kill him as they constrained him to kill Iphigenia. Orestes' guilt is minimal compared with that of Clytemnestra, and even that of Agamemnon, who did, after all, change character and become in the war the destroying eagle of the omen. The Olympians could not leave Orestes to the wrath of Clytemnestra's avengers without surrendering all claim to be the preservers of *dike*.

Nevertheless, Orestes does commit matricide and he is more than the mere hand of Apollo, being also, for a while at least, a willing murderer on his own account. Clytemnestra is not represented as an aggressive enemy who presents him with the choice of killing her or being killed himself. He comes from afar to do the deed. It is by no means certain that she would have planned his death even if he had openly returned—she is not the sheer villainess of Sophocles, who had plotted his end and been foiled by Electra. She had sent him away at least partly in his own interest. Far as Clytemnestra was from being a good woman or justifiable sinner, she was still a mother. Orestes was as much her child as Iphigenia. It is not certain how we are supposed to take the nurse's conviction that Clytemnestra secretly smiled while she pretended to lament the (false) news of his death; she seems to be still the paramour of Aegisthus. But there is no reason to suppose that her desire for peace in the household, which she had expressed at the end of the *Agamemnon*, had changed. This does not mitigate her guilt; it does suggest that she had not abandoned her maternal identity and that Orestes' matricide could not be divested of its personal guilt. Matricide itself was such a horrible thing as to carry with it its own impersonal burden of guilt. It was wrong to kill any mother!

Orestes does commit deliberate matricide and has to overcome a great natural reluctance in order to do so. He falls into the hands of the Erinyes and perpetuates the old chain of violence in his house. But his act is different from that of his predecessors (and especially Clytemnestra), because it (1) has been expressly commanded by Apollo (i.e., the Olympians, including Zeus) and (2) is unjustly avenged by the Erinyes. These are presuppositions of the trilogy. One set of divine actions has to be contradicted by another, one group of gods by another group of gods. Otherwise there can be no justification of Zeus and the Olympians, no solution of the retributive chain of vengeances. The household daimon or daimones cannot be identified with Zeus and Apollo. The "war in heaven" must take precedence over human war, the crimes and guilts of the house of Atreus. This cannot be brought out into the open until we see the plight of Orestes—his divine mission, his human involvement in the matricide and the retribution that follows it and negates the mission.

Orestes is *not* an Agamemnon or Clytemnestra. His guilt cannot justify his punishment, whereas Clytemnestra's guilt can justify even the matricide. All this is the result of Agamemnon's murder; while deserved (Zeus did not feel obliged to establish his *dike* by preventing the murder), it was an outrageous violation of *dike*, an overturning of all political and moral order. It could not be left in the hands of the old daimon or Erinys of the house. It imposed a new strategy on the Olympians. That Clytemnestra is still avenged by the Erinys or Erinyes (the difference of number is significant) implies a complete separation and contradiction of the divine powers. Orestes' personal guilt (as distinct from the retaliation of the Erinys) ceases to be a factor of importance.

Yet it was important up to the murder of Clytemnestra. The horror of matricide could not be easily palliated. This is the right that the Erinyes with some justice defend, or the wrong that they try to punish. Orestes cannot avoid guilt by obeying Apollo as a passive tool, putting all the blame on the god. He has to act as a *son*, an avenger of his father. He is still involved in the house of Atreus and its own retributive justice. It is this situation that constitutes his greatest danger. To submit to matricide too easily, to desire and enjoy the horror of it, to change under the necessity of the deed, might arouse the just retribution that followed Agamemnon's change of character under the "yoke of necessity" that came upon him at Aulis. That Orestes escapes the same fate is due to his character. The kommos shows him steeling himself for the deed

(Schadewaldt) and even beginning to accept its guilt (Lesky), but the moment of action shows that he does *not* accept it, that he has to be urged on by the voice of Apollo speaking through Pylades. He is more than an agent of the god—he shows some personal complicity, but it is minimal, the least possible that Aeschylus' dramatic sense could allow. Lesky, carried away by his rather abstract doctrine of the necessary conjunction of moral responsibility and divine fatality in all of Aeschylus, does not really see this. It is the difference from, not the similarity to, the guilt of Agamemnon with which Aeschylus was here concerned. He shows the difference by emphasizing the similarity: Orestes is not an Agamemnon, even though he encounters a like necessity. While Agamemnon's death is the divine event that has to have this outcome—Orestes has to kill Clytemnestra and be exculpated for the guilt of his act—Orestes must also be given moral freedom. The *Choephoroe* carries its own weight in the trilogy, overwhelming as the weight of the *Agamemnon* is.

Orestes, in the unfortunately truncated prologue, appears with the silent Pylades at Agamemnon's grave. He voices his desire to avenge his father and leaves a lock of his hair as a tribute to the dead. His motive is one of vengeance in general, rather than matricide *per se*. When he sees his sister Electra walking in the posture of bitter grief, he feels a renewed spirit of resentment: ὦ Ζεῦ, δός με τείσασθαι μόρον / πατρός, γενοῦ δὲ σύμμαχος θέλων ἐμοί (18–19). The chorus of female partners (serving-women) of Electra then enters (the parodos) and pronounces its own hope of vengeance. The chorus is "more royalist than the King," the single-minded spur of both Electra and Orestes. Yet even the chorus of the parodos does not face the full fact of matricide; it refers to the "masters" (δεσποτᾶν, 54) of the house in the plural.

The raison d'être of the chorus's entrance is the dream of Clytemnestra. The shrill, hair-raising cry in the night to which the chorus refers (τορὸς . . . ὀρθόθριξ δόμων ὀνειρόμαντις / ἀωρόνυκτον ἀμβόαμα, 32–34) was hers, and caused by her own dream (as yet unrevealed). This has sent the serving-maids and Electra to the tomb with offerings, for the seers have interpreted the dream as an expression of the dead Agamemnon's wrath, and Clytemnestra is vainly trying to avert it. The arrival of Orestes coincides with this prophetic forecast of his vengeance, conceived also as Agamemnon's vengeance on Clytemnestra (for the dream is hers). But Aeschylus, with great dramatic skill, defers the description of the dream to a moment *after* the recognition scene and the ensuing kommos. The dream shows Orestes' evil self, or the evil and matricidal aspect of his vengeance, and corresponds to the eagle omen of the *Agamemnon*. Aeschylus has adapted this portion of the tradition to his own end.

We need not linger over the well-known recognition scene.[3] The warmth of affection between the lonely brother and sister is emphasized to bring out the innocent human emotion before the matricidal motif is developed in the kommos. Electra and Orestes are the lost children of a noble, disgraced father; they are not as yet ready to carry out the vengeance which they still see only in its desirable aspect, as a way out of their present tribulations. They are the "eagle's offspring" whose sire has been crushed in the coils of a dreadful snake (δεινῆς ἐχίδνης, 249). The snake is Clytemnestra, for there is as yet nothing of the snake in Orestes. His explanation of his motives for vengeance is couched almost wholly in terms of Apollo's threatening commands, though he adds that many desires of his own are involved: his grief for Agamemnon, his lost estate and present penury, and the subjection of his house and estate to "two women" (δυοῖν γυναικοῖν, 304), "for Aegisthus has a woman's heart" (θήλεια γὰρ φρήν, 305). There is no moral problem, no hesitation about vengeance on Aegisthus. By coupling him with Clytemnestra, he avoids the full impact of matricide.

The kommos then begins (306). The chorus deliberately turns Orestes' and Electra's attention from Aegisthus (305) to Clytemnestra. The "but" (ἀλλ') of 306 introduces a new phase. Its meaning is: all that Orestes has said is very well, *but* blow must still be given for blow; the doer must suffer (δράσαντα / παθεῖν, 314). This "thrice-old word" (τριγέρων μῦθος, 315) must now be carried out. We can perhaps interpret "thrice-old" as a reference to the house's three retributive crimes (of Atreus, Thyestes, and Agamemnon). In any event the principle of retributive *dike* is asserted. The actual doer—Clytemnestra—is the one who must pay.

After this anapaestic introduction by the chorus (306–14) there follows the kommos proper, consisting of three sets of strophes (each set with three strophes and antistrophes), the first two of which are interlocked in aba'cb'c' order and the last of which is in the order abca'b'c'. The kommos is closed by four strophes (aa', bb'). In the first two sets of triple strophes, the order of speakers is Orestes, chorus, Electra, chorus (an anapaestic interlude), Orestes, chorus, Electra, chorus (another anapaestic interlude); and a repetition of the same speakers in the same order—Orestes, chorus, Electra, chorus (anapaestic interlude), Orestes, chorus, Electra.

3. See Friedrich Solmsen, "Electra and Orestes: Three Recognitions in Greek Tragedy," *Mededelingen der koninklijke nederlandse Akademie*, n.s. 30, 2 (1967) 31–62.

The order of the third set is disputed, since most received texts give it as abcc'a'b' with the speakers arranged in the series chorus, Electra, Orestes, chorus, Electra, chorus. The logic and dramatic force of this decisive part of the kommos (which diverges from the order of strophes or speeches in the first two sets of triple strophes) is here lost. The order abca'b'c' with the speakers arranged as chorus, Electra, chorus, Electra, chorus, Orestes is the only one that corresponds to both the interlocking arrangement of strophes and antistrophes already established *and* the movement of dramatic thought in the kommos. This makes 439–43 the strophe (spoken by the chorus) and 434–38 the antistrophe (spoken by Orestes), which is therefore to be placed *after* the antistrophe a'b' that occurs in 444–55 of present texts.[4]

We can best see the "real" order from the adjoining table. The movement of thought corresponds with almost uncanny exactitude to the movement of the metrical and dramatic elements. The first anapaests (306–13) call Electra and Orestes sternly back to their own task of retribution. Orestes then (315–22) calls on his father to hear and get comfort (χάριτες, 320) from his laments. The chorus, however, insists on the living anger of the dead man and also that the act of mourning reveals the sinner, the murderer:

> τέκνον φρόνημα τοῦ θανόντος οὐ δαμά-
> ζει πυρὸς μαλερὰ γνάθος,
> φαίνει δ' ὕστερον ὀργάς·
> ὀτοτύζεται δ' ὁ θνῄσκων,
> ἀναφαίνεται δ' ὁ βλάπτων.   (324–28)

Electra again begs her father to hear their dirge (θρῆνος, 335), the dirge of exiles and suppliants who have no hope, no chance of contending with their ruinous fate.

The chorus interrupts with anapaests (340–44), opening with another *but* (ἀλλ' ἔτ' ἂν ἐκ τῶνδε θεὸς χρῄζων . . .). *But* the god can change the woeful laments to more mellifluous sounds. There is no reason to despair! Orestes responds with vain wishes: would that his father had died gloriously in Ilium (345–53) and been honorably buried across the sea! He would have been a revered ruler of the dead (σεμνότιμος ἀνάκτωρ, 356), for in life he was a great king. The implication is clear; this is *not* the case. Electra

---

4. See editions by Schütz, Weil, and others. In the most recent critical edition of the text of Aeschylus, *Aeschyli septem quae supersunt tragoedias* (Oxford, 1972), Sir Denys Page says, p. 218: "434–8 post 455 locavit Schütz, manifesto perperam, quamvis mirus sit stropharum ordo ηθι = ιηθ."

Structure of the kommos, with relocation of lines 434–438

Speaker	Lines	Meter
Chorus (introduction)	306–314	anapaests
FIRST SET		
Orestes	315–322 (a)	choriambic dimeters
Chorus	323–331 (b)	iambic trimeters, glyconics, ionics
Electra	332–339 (a′)	choriambic dimeters
Chorus (interlude)	340–344	anapaests
Orestes	345–353 (c)	glyconics, syncopated iambs
Chorus	354–363 (b′)	iambic trimeters, glyconics, ionics
Electra	364–371 (c′)	glyconics, syncopated iambs
Chorus (interlude)	372–379	anapaests
SECOND SET		
Orestes	380–384 (a)	dactyls, choriambs
Chorus	385–393 (b)	choriambs
Electra	394–399 (a′)	dactyls, choriambs
Chorus (interlude)	400–404	anapaests
Orestes	405–409 (c)	syncopated iambs
Chorus	410–417 (b′)	choriambs
Electra	418–422 (c′)	syncopated iambs
THIRD SET		
Chorus	423–428 (a)	iambs
Electra	429–433 (b)	syncopated iambs
Chorus	439–443 (c)	syncopated iambs
Electra	444–450 (a′)	iambs
Chorus	451–455 (b′)	syncopated iambs
Orestes	434–438 (c′)	syncopated iambs
CONCLUSION		
Orestes	456 (a)	syncopated iambs
Electra	457	
Chorus	458–460 (b)	
Orestes	461 (a′)	
Electra	462	
Chorus	463–465 (b′)	
Chorus	466–470 (c)	dochmiacs, choriambs
Chorus	471–475 (c′)	

expresses a contrary but equally impotent wish: would that he had not died at Troy, but destroyed his enemies at home, had murdered and not been murdered by them! The anapaests of the chorus bring them back to reason and reality (371–78). Such wishes are vain! The champions are long since in the earth and the murderers are in control.

$$τῶν μὲν ἀρωγοὶ$$
$$κατὰ γῆς ἤδη, τῶν δὲ κρατούντων$$
$$χέρες οὐχ ὅσιαι †στυγερῶν τούτων·$$
$$παισὶ δὲ μᾶλλον γεγένηται.$$ (376–79)

What could be worse than that?

Orestes (380–85) feels their words like a "shot to the heart." He cries on Zeus for revenge from below, revenge on those who bore him (τοκεῦσι, 385). The chorus wishes for the chance to sing a final alleluia over the dying murderers—the man *and* the woman. Electra calls on Zeus for justice. The law, says the chorus again, is that spilt blood demands blood. The foul murder demands its Erinys: βοᾷ γὰρ λοιγὸς Ἐρινὺν (402). But Orestes shrinks from the deed before him; the present seed of Atreus are helpless and dishonored. Such an attitude shocks the chorus. *But*, it says, his courage will come back and dispel his despair! Electra adds that there can be no beguiling of her mother. She is nothing but a ravening wolf (λύκος γὰρ ὥστ᾽ ὠμόφρων, 421).

The need to act by spilling the actual murderer's blood—even the blood of a mother—has been faced. The next and last triad begins without intervening anapaests; its grim mood is accentuated by the prevailing "strained" iambs. The chorus indulges in cries of mourning (ἔκοψα κομμὸν Ἄριον ἔν τε Κισσίας, 423), where the short syllables show the violence of its emotion. Electra expresses her grievance against her mother: ἰὼ ἰὼ δαΐα / πάντολμε μᾶτερ, (429–30). The terrible shame of Agamemnon's burial at her hands is recalled—no citizens to attend it, no mourning, no grief! Electra does not know the full truth, and the chorus does not shrink from describing the actual horror of the deed (439–43): Clytemnestra's dreadful mutilation of the corpse by cutting off the extremities (especially the genitals) and stringing them under the armpits.[5] Electra now sees what she had missed by being kept in confinement, "like a pestilent dog" (446), at the time. Yet the tale is true. "Hear it and write it in your heart," she warns Orestes. Now, adds the chorus (448–54), "your ears have heard. This is the way it was. It is for you to dare to learn the fierce lesson (τὰ δ᾽ αὐτὸς ὀργᾷ μαθεῖν, 454). Relentless wrath is what befits you now."

5. See Erwin Rohde, *Psyche*[2], vol. 1 (Tübingen and Leipzig, 1897) 322–26, and (London, 1928) 582–86.

Orestes replies by accepting the "lesson":

> τὸ πᾶν ἀτίμως ἔλεξας, οἴμοι.
> πατρὸς δ' ἀτίμωσιν ἆρα τείσει,
> ἕκατι μὲν δαιμόνων,
> ἕκατι δ' ἀμᾶν χερῶν.
> ἔπειτ' ἐγὼ νοσφίσας ὀλοίμαν.   (434–38)

Orestes has faced the necessity of matricide by facing the full horror of his father's disgraceful death and burial. This was entirely his mother's doing. The horror of matricide is still there. His final wish is not the conventional one for the completion of life at the height of success, but a very much more anguished desire to perish rather than face the consequences of his unnatural revenge. As Lesky says, ἔπειτ' ἐγὼ νοσφίσας ὀλοίμαν is an expression of the unlivability of Orestes' situation. Yet in what sense does Orestes here take on the guilt of the vengeance, make the deed his own as well as the gods' responsibility? He does not feel the horrible eagerness of Agamemnon when he accepted the yoke of necessity at Aulis. He feels a new rage, a new ferocity, but against his will, because the facts permit no other reaction. He is not yet hardened. He does not contemplate a long life burdened with the guilt of matricide, even though he accepts and desires the matricide itself. The chorus, which closes the kommos with the reflection that the house of Atreus must save itself without outside help, by its own bloody efforts, can hardly be said to give him much comfort. The kommos ends on an ominous note.

Orestes and Electra now complete their prayers to Agamemnon. They are agreed to avenge him, having seen what vengeance implies. For a moment they revert to an earlier, more human manner in which the kommos and its emotion sink into temporary abeyance. They are once more the children, not the avengers of their father. They are his little fledglings (νεοσσοὺς τούσδ', 501), or the corks that hold up the paternal net, keeping it from sinking in the deep (505–7). They thus recall two key motifs of the *Agamemnon*— the nest bereaved of its fledglings, about which the grief-stricken vultures (Atridae) flew, and the infamous net that had made Agamemnon into a passive victim of his murderess. Here Orestes and Electra are the good against the evil forces of the trilogy, youth and innocence against destructive guile. We recapture the mood of the recognition scene. Tenderness and warmth for a moment displace anger and vengeance; their love for the father, not hatred of his murderess, predominates.

This mood is momentary, a brief contrast. The time, says Electra, has come to act (510–11). Orestes wants to find out the meaning of the offerings at Agamemnon's tomb. What could have induced Clytemnestra to send them? This question opens the way for a description of the dream. Clytemnestra had given birth to a snake, and had nursed it, only to have her breast bitten and her milk mixed with blood. Orestes sees what this means. He is the snake: as she gave him birth and her breast to suck, so now he, in his new serpentine mood, will bite and kill her (ἐκδρακοντωθεὶς δ' ἐγὼ / κτείνω νιν, ὡς τοὔνειρον ἐννέπει τόδε, 549–50).

This is a symbolic clue to the whole drama. Orestes has now (as a result of the kommos) reversed the original snake image. Clytemnestra, the *echidna* who had been described as destroying in her coils the father of the fledglings or young birds (246–49), has now become the victim of a snake. Orestes and Clytemnestra have exchanged roles; good seemingly becomes evil. The analogy of the vultures and the eagles of the *Agamemnon* parodos—first victims of a cruel bereavement, then destroyers in their turn of a defenseless pregnant hare—is relevant. Orestes is under a necessity that seems to change his character. The prophetic dream, which set the play in motion, has now begun to come true. The ambiguity of good and bad, of guilt and innocence, so prevalent in the *Agamemnon*, seems to have come back, the guilt of matricide to have expelled or even overcome the guilt of Agamemnon's death. There is a difference: the dream must originate from the gods; the matricide has been commanded by Apollo; Orestes is not "hardened" in the manner of Agamemnon at Aulis, nor is his intended victim an innocent, divested of her own serpentine characteristics.

The murder plot, unlike that of Sophocles' *Electra*, is simple. Orestes and Pylades, disguised as Phocians, will seek admittance to the palace and, if refused, create such popular sympathy— when it becomes apparent that the royal door is closed against worthy suppliants—that Aegisthus will be shamed into admitting them. Then they will catch him on his throne and kill him: "The Fury, never to be deprived of his blood, will quaff his *third* draft of it" φόνου δ' Ἐρινὺς οὐχ ὑπεσπανισμένη / ἄκρατον αἷμα πίεται τρίτην πόσιν (577–78). We note a strange reluctance to name Clytemnestra, though Orestes in his new serpentine mood will certainly "bite" her.

So ends the long first episode (582). The first stasimon develops the theme of female beastliness. Many indeed are the terrible, fearful evils that earth breeds (πολλὰ μὲν γᾶ τρέφει / δεινὰ δειμάτων ἄχη, 585–86). But who can tell the full tale of human insolence? Of these, the works of female lust are particularly frightful: there is Althea, Scylla, Clytemnestra now! There are the dreadful Lemnian women. But the justice of Zeus stands with poised sword.

Dike and Aisa (Fate) go together: "The famed Erinys of deep purpose is bringing the child to the house to avenge the stain of ancient
blood" (648–51). Two things are notable here, the insistence on
Clytemnestra, on female guilt, on matricide, and thus a solemn
reassertion of the conclusions of the kommos; and the persisting
ambiguity about the divine powers concerned. There is no distinction between Zeus, Fate, and the household Erinys, no separation
of the old crimes of the house of Atreus from the new crime of
Clytemnestra and the anticipated vengeance of Orestes. We have
moved not an inch from the *Agamemnon.*

The next (second) episode is brief (649–778, or 130 lines) but
contains two developments of importance: the reaction of Clytemnestra to the false news of Orestes' death, and the different reaction of his old nurse to the same news. Orestes and the still silent
Pylades knock and are admitted to the palace. Clytemnestra appears. They deliver their message (687–95): "Orestes is dead." At
this, Clytemnestra makes a revealing statement, on which our
judgment of the whole play can be said to turn. To attribute it
to Electra, as Turnebus and later Headlam and Thompson have
done, is to miss its point. Electra does not appear in the episode.
She has already been told by Orestes (579–80) to stay indoors, on
watch; the whole scene takes place before the door of the palace.
(Orestes and Pylades enter at 714, escorted by the servant as directed by Clytemnestra; then the nurse comes out, following a
brief anapaestic interlude of the chorus.) Only Clytemnestra can
be the speaker.

Clytemnestra is not here the hypocritical schemer of the earlier
Agamemnon. Her reaction is in no sense conventional; its sincerity
is not only obvious but striking. In brief paraphrase she says: "I
am now utterly undone. The curse (*ara*) of the house has had its
way. It has envisaged everything, and with far-shooting arrow
deprived me of everything dear. Now it is Orestes—after he had
wisely thought to keep his feet clear of the 'mire' of the house—
who is gone. The last hope of curing the horrible bacchanale in the
house (νῦν δ' ἥπερ ἐν δόμοισι βακχείας κακῆς / ἰατρὸς ἐλπὶς ἦν,
698–99) must be written off as lost (προδοῦσαν ἔγγραφε, 699)."
Clytemnestra expresses her still-subsisting hope for an end to the
chain of crimes—the hope she had expressed to the chorus in the
last kommos of the *Agamemnon.* Orestes as the last survivor of
the house could conceivably have taken over after Aegisthus and
herself, and brought an end to the catastrophic sequence of evils at
Argos. She had tried to save him by sending him to Phocis, and
perhaps wishfully, she had interpreted his continued absence as
his own desire to avoid the "mire" at home. Now all is changed,

and she must take counsel with Aegisthus, the "master" of the house. After the chorus has called upon "deceitful Persuasion" (Πειθὼ δολίαν, 726)—for the plot will turn upon Aegisthus' and Clytemnestra's acceptance of the deceit—the nurse appears. Clytemnestra sent her to summon Aegisthus to the palace. She is Orestes' old nanny, wholly on his side. She interprets Clytemnestra's ostensible grief as an act put on for the benefit of the servants—her face looks sorrowful but her eyes conceal a smile:

> τὴν δὲ πρὸς μὲν οἰκέτας
> θέτο σκυθρωπόν, ἐντὸς ὀμμάτων γέλων
> κεύθουσ' ἐπ' ἔργοις διαπεπραγμένοις καλῶς   (737–39)

We cannot take this as fact. The nurse is only too ready to discount any sincerity in Clytemnestra's words or appearance. Her point of view is confined to the simplest level of physical things and recalls the helpless infant Orestes—the utterly dependent baby—and in a dramatic bit of contrast, sets his recollected infantile innocence against his present vengeance and deception. That she can be used by the chorus (to add to her summons the proviso that Aegisthus come alone without his retinue) indicates the strange reversal of innocence and deception which characterizes the whole passage. Nothing appears quite as it is, neither Clytemnestra's hypocrisy, nor Orestes' innocence, nor the nurse's own simplicity. All is changed and misunderstood. Guile—the snake-like quality, treacherous persuasion—envelops everything.

The second stasimon, which follows the exit of the nurse, envisages the approaching vengeance as a clear expression of the *dike* of Zeus. The rule of *dike* is to be upheld: the avengers want to restore a true morality (δόμου / κυρίοις τὰ σώφρον' αὖ / μαιομένοις ἰδεῖν, 785–87). The old crime is no longer to breed and multiply in the house of Atreus (γέρων φόνος μηκέτ' ἐν δόμοις τέκοι, 806). The approaching deliverance carries with it a happy prospect. An ionic-minor refrain at the end of each strophe and antistrophe equates the matricide with the morality just enounced:

> σὺ δὲ θαρσῶν ὅταν ἥκῃ μέρος ἔργων
> ἐπαύσας θροεούσα
> πρὸς δὲ 'Τέκνον', 'Πατρὸς' αὖδα,
> καὶ πέραιν'
> ἀνεπίμομφον ἄταν.   (827–31)

There is no doubt in the mind of the chorus. The gods and justice are wholly on one side.

The third episode (837–934), of less than a hundred lines, contains the murder and the crisis that reveals the duality of Orestes' motivation—its combination of Olympian and demonic, innocent and serpentine elements. Aegisthus enters, full of his masculine importance and determination not to be hoodwinked. He falls an easy victim; there has never been anything problematic about his guilt. His murder sets up the true drama. A servant sees the deed and cries for help. When Clytemnestra appears, he declares the facts in a transparent riddle ("the living are being killed by the dead") that she quickly reads. It is what she should have expected; "by treachery we are destroyed just as by treachery we killed" (δόλοις ὀλούμεθ᾽, ὥσπερ οὖν ἐκτείναμεν, 888). She asks for an axe; she is prepared "to conquer or be conquered." This is what the past has come to!

When Orestes and Pylades appear with the corpse of Aegisthus, she sees at once the futility of such last-minute bravado. Her mood changes and she makes the famous appeal to Orestes: "Will you strike this bosom that gave you suck?" Not only her act, her exposure of the breast, but her language is here significant:

> ἐπίσχες, ὦ παῖ, τόνδε δ᾽ αἴδεσαι, τέκνον,
> μαστόν, πρὸς ᾧ σὺ πολλὰ δὴ βρίζων ἅμα
> οὔλοισιν ἐξήμελξας εὐτραφὲς γάλα.   (896–98)

Such an action, at such a moment, is enough to dispel all his resolution. He is no longer the vengeful snake. He turns to Pylades beside him and says, Πυλάδη, τί δράσω; μητέρ᾽ αἰδεσθῶ κτανεῖν; (899). This is the crisis of decision. His question provokes the only words that Pylades utters in the entire play: "What then is left of Apollo's oracles? of your own oaths? Make enemies of all men rather than the gods" (900–902). Such advice is enough; after this no words of Clytemnestra can avail. She has preferred Aegisthus to Agamemnon and she must share Aegisthus' fate. Her argument in the *Agamemnon* is turned against her: if her Moira (Fate) caused her to kill his father, her Moira now causes him to kill her. When she cries that she has nourished a snake, he accepts the prophetic truth of her dream in a final acknowledgment of the double evil—the evil she did and the evil he must now do:

> ἦ κάρτα μάντις οὑξ ὀνειράτων φόβος.
> ἔκανες ὃν οὐ χρῆν, καὶ τὸ μὴ χρεὼν πάθε.   (929–30)

The most striking feature of this scene is the dramatic reappearance of Apollo. Apollo's commands had been set forth prior to the kommos. Apollo had played no role—he had not even been mentioned—in the kommos. The divinity at work was the Erinys, the dead man's wrath and curse, the spirit of vengeance at work in his son. Orestes had identified with the Erinys in accepting the snake-role from Clytemnestra's dream. Such motivation had dissolved at the sight of his mother's breast. The necessity of his action had not changed his nature; his matricidal fury had turned out to be impotent.

His appeal to Pylades was to a different source of action. Pylades was no Argive but a neighbor of Delphi, a representative of Apollo. His breaking of his silence at this point can only be understood as divine, an Apolline sign: nothing counted but Apollo and the Olympians! Orestes is not an agent of the Erinys, a domestic *daimon*, but of Apollo. He cannot deny the voice of him who commanded it. He has not lost his filial piety or detestation of Clytemnestra's deeds, above all her disgraceful love for Aegisthus, her wanton adultery; he can even speak in sarcastic terms of her attempt to put the blame on her Moira and her other excuses. But it is Pylades and Apollo who give him the resolution to act. He is now a snake of a different kind. Because she had been a snake—contravening humanity and doing what the necessity of her nature forbade—he must be one. He does what he must, but he does not, in doing it, deny its evil or change character under the yoke of necessity. He acts with his eyes open, his conscience awake.

The third and final stasimon occupies the interval during which the killing of Clytemnestra takes place inside the palace. Its prevailingly dochmiac meter has a tone of wild excitement; the three shorts that begin a large number of the dochmiacs dramatically express the shrill, rapid emotion:

—ἔμολε μὲν δίκα   Πριαμίδαις χρόνῳ,
βαρύδικος ποινά·   (935–36)

There is no doubt in the mind of the chorus that justice has been done, that the house of Atreus has been rid of its evils and crimes. The great bridle-bit has been lifted from it! Apollo's oracles have removed the stain, the chronic ills of the house, by means of Orestes. The blood now being shed will cleanse the house of its sin (*ate*). The chorus, as before, is utterly single-minded, unaware of any conflict of rights or gods.

This elated mood is sustained in the following scene. The doors open and Orestes is revealed standing beside the bodies of Clytemnestra and Aegisthus and holding or pointing to the net or snare in which Agamemnon had been trapped and killed. The setting and Orestes' triumphant speech over the corpses recalls the similar scene and speech of Clytemnestra in the *Agamemnon*. The wheel of justice has come full circle. This is one meaning of the episode, but there is another: that the whole thing is beginning over again, that a new act of vengeance is in the making, now as before, when

Clytemnestra stood in the same place in her own hour of triumph. Orestes dwells on his mother's wickedness. He exposes the dreadful bloodstained net to the sun's light, again refers to her as a snake or snake-like monster:

> τί σοι δοκεῖ; μύραινά γ᾿ εἴτ᾿ ἔχιδν᾿ ἔφυ
> σήπειν θιγοῦσ᾿ ἂν μᾶλλον οὐ δεδηγμένον   (994–95)

But the tone of triumphant hatred is not maintained. In the next few lines Orestes sorrows at his unenviable victory:

> ἀλγῶ μὲν ἔργα καὶ πάθος γένος τε πᾶν,
> ἄζηλα νίκης τῆσδ᾿ ἔχων μιάσματα.   (1016–17)

The chorus, still single-minded and typically uncomprehending, takes this as a general expression of the unavoidable woe in human life. But Orestes is changing. Something has happened to his mind, his emotions: "like stampeded horses, his wits have turned him from his victorious course" (1022). He speaks what he can while he still has some control over himself. He killed his mother in a just cause and at Apollo's command. Now he can only become a bloodstained exile from his country, with no hearth open to him but Apollo's.

The chorus again fails to understand. Why such evil words, when he is the deliverer (1046) of Argos? Has he not cut off the heads of two snakes? These words of the chorus only point to the horror it cannot see. It is quite another sort of snake that appears to Orestes' bewildered eyes: "What women these, like Gorgons black and thick entwined with snakes?" (1048). The chorus cannot see what he sees. There are no "raging hounds of his mother" (1054) around; it is the blood on his hands that has confused his wits. But the blood Orestes sees is that which drips from the horrible eyes of the Furies. He can do nothing but flee in frenzied horror. His vengeance has begotten a new vengeance, one more link in the seemingly unbreakable chain of Argive crimes. The only hope, but not a very satisfactory one, which the chorus now exressses, is that "Apollo's touch will make him free of his woes" (τῶνδε πημάτων, 1060). A third storm has broken over the house of Atreus: the Thyestean banquet, the murder of Agamemnon, now this! Is it salvation or destruction? When will it all end? When will such calamity (*ate*) ever be put to sleep?

This reversion to the wickedness of the house—the self-perpetuating chain of guilt and blood—strikes a new note in the play. We had forgotten the crimes of Thyestes and Atreus, the hereditary aspect of Orestes' matricide. Apollo had seemingly taken charge and the Erinys had been relegated to the dim background.

We now see that the old Erinyes are still at work and that Orestes too is enveloped in their inescapable toils. This time the "doer" does not bear the whole responsibility or share it with his own amoral Erinys. His decisive reversion to the authority of Apollo at the time of the matricide has put the Olympians on his side and made their justice his own. They cannot allow the avenger to become the object of another vengeance.

The play as a whole is well adapted to the purpose that Aeschylus had in mind. This has often been misunderstood. The essential conflict is not between Orestes and Clytemnestra or Aegisthus, but between Apollo and the *daimon* or Erinys of the house of Atreus. Orestes appears under the aegis of Apollo (Pylades is really Apollo's human representative) to act as Apollo's agent of justice. His encounter with Electra and her partisan handmaidens is beset by a spirit of revenge. Apollo is absent from the kommos; the appeal is to the dead Agamemnon, to his ghost or the Erinys of the Atridae raging for vengeance, though the chorus does not distinguish this from the justice of Zeus himself. Here Orestes encounters the true horror of matricide and the horror—the frightful burial and dismemberment of his father's body—that seems to justify it. Lesky is so far right: at this point Orestes changes under the necessity of vengeance into a voluntary matricide. He accepts the role of the snake that bites the maternal breast. He no longer sees himself as the child of the snake's victim, but rather Clytemnestra as the victim of her snake-child. The serpentine roles have shifted from one to the other side.

Orestes cannot sustain the new role: at the crisis he falters and cannot bite his mother's exposed bosom. Apollo once more speaks through the mouth of Pylades and restores the original reality. Orestes becomes the snake, but with the responsibility now shared by the god. Orestes has not yet come to terms with himself; he is still both justified and guilty. His attempt to repeat the scenario of Agamemnon—the corpses, the net, the open avowal of the deed's justice—is deflated by a mood of sorrow and anguish, a horrible paralysis of will, and finally by the presence of the Erinyes. Only Apollo can help him now!

It is the matricide that constitutes Orestes' problem and the problem of the play. The proper course would have been to avoid it. There is some reason to think that once Aegisthus had been disposed of, Clytemnestra would have submitted and accepted the rule of Orestes. She could have been exiled or relegated to an obscure retreat in Argos. There is no indication that she hated Orestes or wanted to murder him. But such a solution is prohibited from the start. She must pay for her crime. Agamemnon

must be avenged. Apollo has so ordained. The actual temper of
Clytemnestra—the enigmatic indications of regret for Orestes'
apparent death—plays a very minor role. She remains his mother.
To kill her is to submit to the old Erinys of vengeance, to prolong
the horrors of the house, to accept the blood-guilt of a matricide. The household Erinys had worked through such a displace-
ment of normal humanity, by hardening the spirit against the
demands of conscience and of natural feeling. So had it once
worked in Agamemnon and, in much greater degree, in Atreus
and Clytemnestra.

Orestes is different. After the kommos he had seemed to be following the same path—though with much greater justification—
but he had at the last moment overcome his matricidal passion, the
sheer spirit of blood-vengeance, the old Erinys in short, and re-
verted to his role as Apolline agent and representative. He was still
covered with blood-guilt; the Erinyes appeared, the bloodhounds
of his mother were tracking him down. This could not be for
his own responsibility. That united front of all the supernatural
powers—the joint implementation of justice—of which the chorus
had been so confident, is now seen to be illusory. The reality was a
"war in heaven," a war between the chthonic and the Olympian
powers.

One of the most interesting things about the play is its de-
emphasis of the killing of Aegisthus and Clytemnestra. It is certain
that they must and will die. The important question is how they
will die. The tension that surrounded the murder of Agamemnon
cannot be repeated: the decisive break with the past came with it,
and the rest was its consequence. A new stage in the criminal
history of the Atridae occurred. A new clarity dissipated the old
obscurity. Orestes acts with Olympian credentials. But how does
this alter the meaning of his act? Does Apollo in effect take the
place of the house Erinys or cooperate with the old Erinys and
provoke another spasm of blood-lust and murderous ecstasy? Does
Orestes assume the soul or feelings of a matricide? Only the decisive confrontation with his mother can answer that question,
though the kommos and the dream (the reversed snake-motif)
have led us to anticipate the answer. But the answer we anticipate is shown to be wrong: Orestes obeys Apollo. The problem
of Orestes' motive becomes secondary. The question is one of
Apollo's justification. Was he right in commanding the matricide?
Can he control the spirits who try to avenge it?

The distinction between Apollo and the *daimon* or Erinys of the
house had been left in obscurity. The *Agamemnon* had suggested a
distinction, since there was an implicit difference between the

spirit of primitive vengeance that had caused the Thyestean banquet, and the murder of Agamemnon and the justice of Zeus. Both
sides demanded vengeance on Clytemnestra. There is not the least
hint, before the very end of the *Choephoroe*, that the one side was
interested only in the maternal, the other in the paternal line. To
the chorus, Zeus and the Erinys are in complete accord. Orestes
sees no opposition between the vengeance called for by the chorus
in its appeal to the Erinys of Agamemnon and that demanded of
him by Apollo. The horror of matricide is of the same texture as
the horror of the other crimes of his house. Aeschylus could solve
his problem only by making some kind of distinction between the
supernatural powers. This is not dramatically evident until Orestes
and Apollo have experienced the distinction. When the Erinyes
appear against both Orestes and Apollo, the die has been cast.
Both sides cannot be right, or the two rights must be brought into
a definite and clear relationship through which effective human
justice can be done.

And there were two rights. Orestes' horror of matricide was
justified; so was his acceptance of it. It is this conjunction and
discrepancy of motives and feelings that makes the play. Clytemnestra is evil, but it is evil to kill her. The simple revenge theme of
the kommos is included within the context of the dream—the
dream that begins the play by sending Electra and the chorus to
the tomb and is fulfilled ($\tau\varepsilon\lambda\varepsilon\sigma\phi\delta\rho\sigma\nu$, 541) when Orestes in person
enacts the snake. Orestes cannot exchange roles with Clytem-
nestra, who is the original and primary snake of the trilogy. He
cannot be permitted to bear the full onus of the matricide. By
throwing it upon Apollo, he solves the human problem of the
trilogy, or transcends the heretofore inescapable conjunction of
personal moral guilt and outer or divine necessity. He takes the
great step beyond Agamemnon and his predecessors and frees
himself from personal responsibility and retribution. Apollo and
Zeus now have to act, to end a system of which even matricide
seemed a necessary concomitant.

The Furies are not immoral or wicked powers. Nor is Apollo a
simple equivalent of justice. The delimitation of the Furies to a
special kind of vengeance—within the bloodline—is a narrowing
of a special aspect of the old retributive justice. The Olympians
had not heretofore interfered and in fact had cooperated with it.
How could they expect the older powers to accept their present intervention? Their answer to the old system of justice could only be
a new system of justice. No unilateral act by Apollo could suffice.
Men had accepted the tacit complicity of Furies and Olympians
either by justifying their divine or external motivation through

their human and personal guilt or by changing from good to evil under the yoke of necessity. It is this that Orestes does not do.

One reason why the respective rules of gods and men can be clarified at this point is that Clytemnestra has no living human descendant who could avenge her: her actual children, Electra and Orestes, are themselves murderers. This forces the *daimones* or Erinyes to intervene in person and not through another human being. Since Clytemnestra has been the victim of Apollo, the Erinyes must oppose him. A reason has to be given for their action, a disclosure of their nature and rationale. Heretofore the Moira, Ara, *daimon*, or Erinys (usually described in the singular) has been the spirit of vengeance and blood-lust, motivated by a certain justice, or *dike*, but in such a way that a further act of bloody *dike* or *tisis* was required. Guilt produced guilt; vengeance, vengeance—without end or respite. "The doer must pay": that and only that, is the "thrice-old word" of the house of Atreus. The connection of Zeus and the Olympians with all this had been veiled in obscurity. How could men ever "learn wisdom by suffering" under such conditions? Artemis and Zeus were the causes of Agamemnon's sacrifice of Iphigenia and even of Clytemnestra's own crimes. The chorus at the end of the *Agamemnon* had expressed its conviction that Zeus was the cause and agent of all that had happened (ἰὼ ἰὴ διαὶ Διὸς / παναιτίου πανεργέτα, 1485–86), but it had also expressed its horror of the terrible *daimon* or Erinys of the house and its despair of a reconciling solution. Not only the conjunction of Zeus and the *daimon*, but the conjunction of their action with the personal guilt of their human agents, seemed to constitute a impenetrable unity of tragic fate.

The *Choephoroe* has separated or split these two conjunctions into an intelligible and reconcilable opposition. Zeus is no longer at one with the *daimon* or Erinys. And Orestes is no longer the agent of the *daimon* of revenge. He had shown this by his action at the crisis of the play when he saw that only Apollo could justify his matricide. Unlike Agamemnon, he did not change character and desire the dreadful necessity of his deed. It is this that Lesky's brilliant discussion of the kommos has obscured.

The four episodes of the play are of uneven length. The first has 501 lines; the second, 130; the third, 93; the last, 104. The parodos has 62 lines; the great kommos of the first episode, 172; the first stasimon, 67; the second stasimon, 54; the third stasimon, 48. The parodos and stasima together make 231 lines against the 172 of the kommos. In the *Agamemnon*, the long parodos (220 lines) and first two stasima (136 and 103 lines) enclose relatively short episodes (95 and 192 lines). The proportion of parodos and stasima to epi-

sodes is 459 to 287 lines, or almost two to one—and more than half
the play is yet to come. The points of emphasis are the Cassandra
kommos, the murder, and the kommos of chorus and Clytemnestra
(fourth episode and exodus). The *Choephoroe* reverses the arrangement of the *Agamemnon*. In the former, the point of lyric-dramatic
intensity—where the lyrical and dramatic elements fuse—is the
Electra-Orestes-chorus kommos, quite early in the play; in the
Agamemnon the point of similar intensity is late in the play with the
Cassandra kommos, which prolongs the "present" of the murder.
The murder in the *Choephoroe* is anticipated by the kommos and
the dream (the two major structural elements of the first episode).
The stasima are shorter and more static; they progress—they are
not "ring compositions"—but they do not build up tension in the
manner of the *Agamemnon* or extend a vast panorama of past events
into a dramatic present.

The *Choephoroe* is concerned with a more specific issue (the past
has been discounted by Agamemnon's death): the decision of
Orestes to commit matricide, his position between the Erinys of
the house (or familial vengeance) and the commands of Apollo.
The murder—whose fatality is heavily discounted—shows on
whose side Orestes would act. It is his new Apolline identity that
gives the exodos its tragic and frenetic character: the real problem
has passed into the divine sphere, and Orestes is now no more
than a pathetic victim. The last two episodes bring to a head all
that has been foreshadowed and built up before. Without the
factors that bear on Orestes' decision to commit matricide, the
murder itself would be meaningless. (In the *Agamemnon*, the motivation and guilt of Clytemnestra's action are never in doubt; the
problem is what it will mean, how it can sum up the past and settle
the future.)

Orestes' guilt is a question affecting both human and divine
reality. The murder is the dotting of i's and the crossing of t's.
Orestes' Apolline motivation must be asserted, but that would
have meant little had we not seen the frightful burden of matricide
as it grew upon his shoulders. This is the raison d'être of the
kommos and the dream-motif and the human solidarity of the
brother and sister. This is unintelligible to the single-minded and
determined chorus. The play is a drama of motivation, and it is
arranged with everything centered on the manner or motive, not
the fact, of Orestes' action. Since Orestes is not guilty like his
predecessors, the justice of his action can be vindicated in a way
that cuts off the possibility of any further guilt or retribution.

V. THE *EUMENIDES*

There is no need to discuss the *Eumenides* in similar detail. It answers the question presented at the end of the *Choephoroe*. The two "rights" are harmonized and Zeus' *dike* prevails in the form and jurisdiction of the homicide court of Athens, the Areopagus. Orestes is acquitted and the demon-breeder of crimes at Argos is finally put to sleep. But the fundamental problems—the discrepancy between the bloodthirsty primitive powers and the wisdom or justice of Zeus, the enigmatic conjunction of personal responsibility and divine necessity in human action—are not given what we would call a satisfactory solution. The delimitation of the activity of the Erinyes to crimes in the blood, or the direct line, does distinguish them from the Olympians (Apollo), as is essential for the ensuing determination and accommodation of the rights involved, but it hardly accounts for all the catastrophes of the house of Atreus. Clytemnestra avenged Iphigenia; Aegisthus avenged Thyestes; Orestes avenged Agamemnon on both Aegisthus and Clytemnestra. Nothing indicates that the *daimones* or Erinyes mentioned by Cassandra would have failed to avenge the murder of Agamemnon, and much indicates that this is what they did in the shape of Orestes himself. The indifference of the Erinyes to Agamemnon's fate seems a belated development. Their specialized view of blood-guilt distracts attention from the basic equity of the case and forces Apollo to advance the curiously perverse plea that mothers have no proper share in their children since they are merely recipients of the father's seed. It is not the justification of matricide but the setting up of a system that will prevent it and other crimes that constitutes the real raison d'être of the Areopagus. To oppose father-right to mother-right is to confuse the moral issue altogether.

In one sense the *Eumenides* is superficial in both its theodicy and its morality; in another it reveals its own peculiar profundity. Apollo, when he takes charge of Orestes, disassociates himself from the demons of the house and from their amoral bloodthirsty ways. Once this dissociation has taken place, the opposition of rights makes evident the necessity of their reconcilation and results in a justice fully expressive of the will of Zeus. The Erinyes punish the matricide but not the husband-killing woman. The matricide was wrong *per se*, but right in that it punished a greater wrong.

Nevertheless it was not a just way of dealing with family and civic guilt. Such vengeful punishment had to be taken out of the hands of the family (and the gods of the family) and entrusted to Zeus and Athena and the divine court they established. This transformation of the older, cruder justice, or law of retribution, is also a continuation of it. There are still two rights—the older one of the Erinyes and the newer one of the Olympians—and though the latter was the better, the former cannot be suppressed.

The two peculiarities of the play that strike the modern reader as strange or grotesque—the amoral delimitation of the Erinyes' rule and Apollo's curious apology for matricide—are both required by the logic of the trilogy. Some way of distinguishing the levels of deities, the primitive from the Olympian, some argument that would not simply refute the morality of the primitive forces, the Furies, could have solved Aeschylus' problem. There is more right on Orestes' side: the murder of Agamemnon had altered the terms in which the guilt question had been discussed; the palpable evil of Clytemnestra's action forced both men and gods to demand a new kind of justice. The question was not the moral superiority of the Olympians—that was ambiguous. Apollo is full of moral ambiguity: he sees nothing wrong in the matricide he commands; he deprives the Furies of their rights; he thinks of the issue largely in terms of masculine prerogative. He thereby puts himself on a level that permits the justice of the Furies to seem less partial. Accordingly, the vote of the jury is evenly divided. The attitude of Athena—though she is in accord with Apollo's views—is different. Instead of loathing and despising the Furies, she treats them as potential friends. Whatever we may say of the passages in which the wills of Apollo, Zeus, and Athena are practically identified, the differentiation of Apollo's and Athena's roles in the play is of great dramatic significance. That Apollo is so partisan and indiscriminating, so sophistic and dubious a pleader, equalizes the arguments and permits Athena to preserve the appearance of a judicial impartiality, to maintain a position above the battle and consequently to effect a final reconciliation.

Here we must see the influence of Hesiod's *Theogony*.[1] The Hesiodic opposition of the "older" to the "newer" gods and amalgamation of the two under the single reign of Zeus, or in more general terms the old Creation story that goes far back into primitive antiquity (the contest of Marduk and Tiamat in the Babylonian Creation epic *Enuma Elish* is but one version of it), is here brought into dramatic conjunction with both Mycenaean mythology and

1. See Friedrich Solmsen, *Hesiod and Aeschylus* (Ithaca, 1949).

mid–fifth-century democratic practice. At a decisive moment the older and newer gods come into conflict, and out of this conflict divine and political peace ensue. The foundation of the democratic Areopagus stopped the begetting of one sin by another and reconciled the older and primitive with the newer and democratic justice. This was a divine act motivated by the injustice and horror of Agamemnon's death. Because his death was conceived as a cosmic event that had divided the gods or brought their division to a crisis, the validity of Zeus' rule was at stake.

The drama is not about the rights of blood kinship or of male versus female, but about Zeus and *dike*. The older *dike* was both good and bad, and obscure. Zeus' relation to it was at best doubtful, at worst deceptive. The Hesiodic division and succession of the gods became the key myth by which the necessary change in this intolerable situation could be brought about. The explanation of the division—the difference between gods concerned with crimes in the bloodline and those concerned with crimes not in the bloodline—is of secondary importance. Aeschylus' linking of a moment in Argive-Mycenaean legend with a moment of Hesiodic change and a moment of political change (from monarchy to democracy) was the imaginative feat that made this drama possible: a single decisive act (the murder of Agamemnon) broke through one divine-human *status quo* and set up another. Only by such an act could political *dike* and the rule of Zeus overcome the powers that had resisted them.

A brief recapitulation of the play will make this clear. The first 234 lines (prologue and, technically, part of the first episode) are set in Delphi, the rest of the drama in Athens. This unusual change of venue is of great significance. It tells us that Apollo by himself could not solve Orestes' problem, that more was needed than the purification of blood-guilt that was his special function. One will seriously misunderstand the play—indeed the trilogy— if one assumes that Aeschylus changed the locale because of his own Athenian loyalties. The issue is one between Apollo, or all the Olympians, and quite other gods—the Furies—and more is needed to settle it than a mere assertion of one-sided power. In Stesichorus' *Oresteia*, Apollo, so we are informed, lent Orestes his bow in order to allow him to ward off or get rid of the Furies.[2] This was no way of terminating a trilogy concerned with essential questions of *dike* and its relation to Zeus. If the Furies were not to

2. D. L. Page, *Poetae Melici Graeci* (Oxford, 1962) Stesichorus 217.13–32; Eduardus Schwartz, ed., *Scholia in Euripidem*, vol. 1 (Berlin, 1887) 126, scholia to *Orestes* 286.1.

be dealt with by force majeure, which would have obliterated the older right and denied any kind of previous justice, they had to be made to submit by peaceful means. The Athenian Areopagus—or in more general terms the impersonal or impartial public justice of the *polis*—was thus able to supply what Apollo (or his shrine) could not. Delphi was not an independent *polis* like Athens. Athena could not play a role like Apollo's. The court's decision could not convert the Furies, but it represented a step toward their conversion. Had Athena acted like Apollo and attempted only to threaten the Furies, she could hardly have persuaded them to change.

What we see in the part of the play set in Delphi is the dramatic confrontation of the two sets of gods and the unhappy intermediate position of Orestes. The Hesiodic opposition of old and new regimes is made explicit: we now discover what the ending of the *Choephoroe* meant. The opening contrast between the august and pure *prophetis*—with her solemn prayer to the Olympians before she enters the temple—and the horrible Furies that she finds inside it and flees from in loathing and terror, strikes the keynote of the play: the emotional distance, the repulsion and antagonism which divides the two sets of gods. When the doors of the temple open and we see the Furies surrounding Apollo, Hermes, and Orestes, we receive the shock we have been prepared for by the reactions of the *prophetis*; but the shock is muted, for the fearful-looking goddesses are still asleep. Apollo's attitude toward them is not one of terror, like that of the *prophetis*, but of hatred and loathing: "abominable maidens, old women like aged children, with whom no god nor man nor beast associates, begotten for evil's sake, dwelling in the darkness and Tartarus beneath the earth, hated by all mankind and the Olympian gods" (69–73).

The scene reveals the extent to which the real opposition—the dramatic clash of characters—has passed from the human to the divine level. Apollo fully admits his responsibility for Orestes' act: καὶ γὰρ κτανεῖν σ᾿ ἔπεισα μητρῷον δέμας (84). Orestes, in his brief three-line acknowledgment of Apollo's aid, appears as a complete dependent, an all but will-less personality who can only do what Apollo tells him and hope for the best. Apollo, he says, knows what is just (οἶσθα μὲν τὸ μὴ ἀδικεῖν, 85), and should not neglect it (καὶ τὸ μὴ ἀμελεῖν μάθε, 86). Apollo by himself cannot free Orestes from the Furies' pursuit. Here Aeschylus breaks with the traditional myth. All that Apollo can do is to take advantage of the Furies' temporary slumber and send off Orestes under Hermes' guidance to Athens and the intervention of Athena. Once there, he will be freed from his woes by "judges" (δικαστὰς, 81) and "persuasive words" (θελκτηρίους μύθους, 81–82). It is not until

Orestes has left the temple and, presumably, Delphi, that the Furies awake, under the goading of the implacable ghost of Clytemnestra, and come into a direct confrontation with Apollo.

Clytemnestra's call for aid on her protective divinities is more peremptory and shows a strength and self-confidence materially different from the dazed helplessness of Orestes. No deity, she says, is angry for her, matricidally slaughtered as she was! She will allow them no respite in their implacable pursuit of Orestes, and insists that it is up to them to defend their prerogatives against Apollo. Their slumber is a trick of Apollo which has allowed their victim to escape. Their opening chorus—which is no ordinary parodos or entrance, for they are already at hand—states the essential opposition of forces. Apollo is the thief (ἐπίκλοπος, 149) who tramples on his elders. This is the sort of thing that the new gods are doing (τοιαῦτα δρῶσιν οἱ νεώτεροι θεοί, 162). They are trying to overthrow all justice and loyalty (κρατοῦντες τὸ πᾶν δίκας πλέον, 163), and Apollo's regard for mortals has broken the divine law (παρὰ νόμον θεῶν βρότεα μὲν τίων, 171).

The conflict of gods and rights breaks into the open when Apollo returns and roughly tells the Furies to leave his temple. He is no mere abettor of Orestes, they cry, "he himself is the doer, the criminal" (200). Apollo does not deny his responsibility: he did tell Orestes to avenge his father—what of it? But this, the Furies say, is to make himself responsible for "new blood" (κἄπειθ᾽ ὑπέστης αἵματος δέκτωρ νέου, 204). "Not without absolution for it," Apollo rejoins. Absolution, however, (προστραπέσθαι, 205) is not sufficient to save Orestes. The Furies' function (τιμή, 209) is to hunt down matricides, and Orestes is a matricide. The crime of Clytemnestra does not concern them, because it does not affect their own province, murder in the direct bloodline (ὅμαιμος αὐθέντης φόνος, 212). What is to Apollo murder deserving punishment is not their business; what to them is murder, also deserving punishment, is to Apollo justice and therefore not "new blood" demanding further punishment. If they, Apollo tells them, do not pursue the violators of the marriage bed, the sacred Zeus-honored bond of wife and husband, then their pursuit of Orestes is unjust.

We cannot refrain from asking what would have happened if the Furies had pursued *both* Clytemnestra and Orestes or if, as seems to have been their role in the house of Atreus, the Furies had worked within each link, or human agent, in the chain of successive vengeances. Apollo's intervention to avenge this particular murder was an exception to prior practice in which the Olympians either did not interfere or cooperated with the Erinyes. What differentiates this case from the others is the spectacular injustice

of Clytemnestra's action and the moral indifference to it of the
Erinyes. It is not that husband-killers are as bad as mother-killers
and deserve an equal justice, but that in this case the husband-
killer has caused the respective gods in question to react in a new
way. The unilateral motivation of Apollo (the Olympians) is the
obverse of the unilateral right or law of the Erinyes. But this right
was unknown or utterly obscure until Apollo intervened. It is the
morally unequal character of their νόμος or τιμή (law or function)
that goes with the ferocity and bloodthirstiness of their nature.
They are not moral or just, because they are not humane, not
interested in civilized life. Their outlook is fierce and narrow.
Apollo cannot alter it. He does not attempt to persuade them; he
deliberately provokes them. Other hands than his must settle the
quarrel if it is to be settled at all. Its cosmic or Hesiodic character
begins to emerge—the profound opposition of two generations of
gods.

The rest of the play can be treated in summary fashion. The
first Athenian pronouncement of the Furies, as they enter the
Areopagus to find Orestes clinging for protection to the image of
Athena, defines their attitude in a more moral fashion. They assert
a threefold function: to punish all who do evil to gods, to strangers,
and to parents (ἢ θεὸν ἢ ξένον / τιν' ἀσεβῶν ἢ τοκέας φίλους, 270–
71). They do play a moral or ethical role and their motivation is
not mere bloodthirstiness. This sharpens their opposition to Zeus:
why has he denied their special and just prerogatives? It is the
limitedness of their prerogatives (whether moral or not) that is in
question. As Athena reminds them, they seek the appellation, not
the reality of justice (κλύειν δικαίως μᾶλλον ἢ πρᾶξαι θέλεις, 430).
They are concerned with "half the case" (ἥμισυς λόγου, 428).
Athena herself (and inferentially the Olympians) cannot decide
the *whole* case. When she says that it is too great a matter (τὸ
πρᾶγμα μεῖζον, 470) for mortals to decide, and even she herself
cannot rightly (οὐδὲ μὴν ἐμοὶ θέμις, 471) judge so terrible a suit of
blood (φόνου διαιρεῖν ὀξυμηνίτου δίκας, 472), and one involving so
humble and pure a suppliant, she is not referring so much to the
intrinsic difficulty of the case as to the fact that the Furies are, as
she says, pitiless and determined to lay waste the city if they do
not win it. This is the great evil to avoid, and the court is set up to
be the means to this end. The issue, as she adds, is doubtful, but
one that only impartial justice can hope to resolve.

True justice demands the setting up in perpetuity of an impartial
court. This court is not regarded as simply human—the matter is
beyond mortal cognizance—or even simply divine. Neither set of
gods can control it, but something above both sides. Thus there

is a sense—never very clearly expressed—in which Zeus stands above the battle. He clearly agrees with Athena and, in appearance at least, with Apollo, but he is also the supreme, transcendent god whose justice is deeper and less partial than that of the lesser deities and identical with the justice of the new court.

The second stasimon, before the trial, reinforces the morality of the Furies with a more direct and generalized emphasis on justice. There is only a fleeting reference to matricide; what is particularly insisted on is the rule of law (μήτ' ἄναρκτον βίον / μήτε δεσποτούμενον / αἰνέσῃς, 526–28), and the negative demand for punishment is balanced by an insistence on the reward of the just. The Furies express an ethic that is fully as high as any in the choruses of the *Agamemnon* or *Choephoroe*. They are already well on the way toward acceptance of the new political justice. It is wrong to attribute complete consistency to the Furies in this play or in the whole trilogy: they change as the moment of the trial draws near.

The Furies stand for a justice as valid as Apollo's. That their νόμος or τιμή was a partial justice, as Athena had already declared, did not cancel or destroy the fact that it was justice, because it followed an inflexible rule, a rigid application of principle, limited though that principle might be from the standpoint of a broader principle. Apollo had intervened in a single case, had not acted by an established law or inflexible rule. He had committed himself to neither the old justice of the kin group nor the new justice of the *polis*. If his action was just in one sense, it was unjust in another. A new rule was needed, a rule that would supersede that of the Erinyes and extend the single intervention of Apollo into a new but similarly inflexible justice. This logic demanded a cooperative association, a fusion of forces, between the Erinyes and Apollo, between their partial but inflexible justice and his arbitrary, or single-case justice.

Aeschylus saw in the Athenian Areopagus the perfect symbol of the new, cooperative rule. The Areopagus is divine beyond all previous conceptions of divinity. It stands for the justice of Zeus, which supersedes the justices of both the Furies and Apollo. On the human level it is designed to supersede the familial justice of murders and the unbreakable chain of violence that this entailed. The *polis* and the united gods of the *polis* take over from the individual and the family. Neither Apollo nor the Furies will any longer commission private or familial avengers or involve them in the guilt that was so mysteriously united with their divine necessity, but will leave vengeance to a court, to the *polis*, to its collective and divinely established institutions.

The trial seems to us, on first reading at least, to be anticlimactic. When we might have expected Apollo as counsel for Orestes to have advanced a definitive defense of the pure justice of his case, he puts himself on the same level as the Furies and advances a case for the superior right of males and fathers as opposed to females and mothers. He refers to the sheer horror of Agamemnon's murder, but he avoids the ethical question. His procedure is explicable when we consider its relation to the importance of the impartiality of the court. Aeschylus does not want Apollo to score an obvious victory. The Furies are not now represented as simple enemies of justice, and the point is to reconcile, not alienate them. The issue has gone beyond the mere acquittal of Orestes. The text seems to indicate that even Athena's casting vote only equalizes the ballot count.[3] As she declares, that is all she needs to win: νικᾷ δ' Ὀρέστης, κἂν ἰσόψηφος κριθῇ (741). Even if this is not the case, the even division of the human ballots indicates the intention of Aeschylus here: impartial justice is done; both sides have been assured of their right, and the decision is as close as possible to a justification of each. There is no attempt to assert an antagonistic moral superiority. There are still two rights, two justices.

This and the general attitude of Athena makes the reconciliation possible. The long epirrhema, or exchange of iambic trimeter and lyric responses, between Athena and the chorus is not a progressive line of argument (unlike those of the *Choephoroe* and *Agamemnon* kommoi), but a persistent wearing down of an idée fixe (the Furies' former *persona*) by the ironic determination of Athena. Because she has shown her concern for impartial justice, her voice can be persuasive. The familial, political, and cosmic turn of events set in motion by the murder of Agamemnon have finally come to a happy ending and a new, better, juster condition of things among both gods and men. Beside this, Orestes, Agamemnon, and Clytemnestra shrink to secondary importance. The human act—the murder of Agamemnon—has been dwarfed by its consequences.

3. Michael Gargarin, "The Vote of Athene," *American Journal of Philology* 96 (1975) 121–27.

Does the *Oresteia* reveal the true Aeschylus? Is the tragedy presented by the *Agamemnon* a new development or just another example of Aeschylean dramatic art? Our argument has been that the problem of Agamemnon's guilt was soluble only by a new dispensation in which the necessary conjunction of human responsibility and divine causation was replaced by a different divine-human relationship, one in which the older, quasi-automatic working out of guilt and vengeance was subsumed in a clear-cut human justice guaranteed by cooperating deities. The guilt of Agamemnon and its consequences belong to the old regime, and the murder of Agamemnon is the decisive act that breaks up the old regime and brings in the new. This gives the tragedy of Agamemnon its peculiar character and determines its peculiar technique. The *Choephoroe* and *Eumenides*, as consequences of the *Agamemnon*, were bound to possess a different character and technique. The murder of Clytemnestra plays a different role and has a different dramatic function from that of Agamemnon, and the *Eumenides* is the nontragic resolution of both.

The prevailing view of the *Oresteia* as a more or less uniform work in which the choral pronouncements of the *Agamemnon* are applicable to the whole trilogy and all guilts are judged in similar terms—the view that the moral obscurity of the *Agamemnon*, and particularly of its earlier portions, is not clarified by the murder and its consequences so that a 'Hesiodic' change occurs—is not only an incorrect interpretation of the whole trilogy, but a definite bar to our understanding of the *Agamemnon*.

Its tragedy is not a typical expression of human blindness (like the *Oedipus*) or the occasion for a pathetic effect (as in Euripides), but an agent of cosmic change. This is why its drama or action is *sui generis*, why the choruses, episodes, and kommoi are so differently conceived and arranged, why each part of the play has to be understood in terms of its dramatic location. Neither spectators nor chorus know, at the outset or in the parodos of the *Agamemnon*, what is the wisdom that Zeus teaches by suffering, because Zeus himself has not yet taught it. The suffering of Agamemnon not only illustrates a moral principle, it sets in motion the events

which create a new moral principle and clarify the ambiguity of
the old principle. There is a difference between cosmic tragedy—
the tragedy that is cosmic change, change from an old to a new
dispensation—and tragedy that is simply one more illustration of
the "doubtful doom" of mankind. How far is the *Oresteia*, on this
exegesis, consistent with the earlier plays of Aeschylus? Here the
accident that we possess only seven out of seventy or more plays,
and only one of at least a score of trilogies, precludes a definite
answer.

One fact, however, makes an answer easier than the absence of
data would indicate. The discovery of a papyrus fragment of the
Suppliants fixing the date at 466 B.C. or after, in all probability at
463,[1] separates the extant plays of Aeschylus into two categories.
The known date of the *Oresteia* (458) and the probable lateness of
the *Prometheia* (460 or later) fix these plays as subsequent to the
Septem contra Thebas, or the Labdacid trilogy (467) of which it was
the final part (*Laius* and *Oedipus* are now lost). The *Persae* (472) is
the only surviving earlier play. The plays between 484 (Aeschylus'
first victory or the beginning of his *akme*) and 472 are either lost
or preserved in such insignificant fragments that any discussion
of them is bound to be hypothetical. The *Persae* is not part of a
trilogy. The essential comparison is between the *Septem* (fortu-
nately for us the last or resolving play of its trilogy) and the later
plays (*Suppliants, Oresteia, Prometheus*). Can we see any common
features that would differentiate them from the *Septem* or associate
them with each other as a special group? There are seven years
between the probable date of the *Suppliants* (463) and Aeschylus'
death (456). If the *Prometheia* belongs in this period, we have the
parts at least of three trilogies produced over only seven years.
These must have constituted a full half of Aeschylus' production
in that time span, and in all probability much more than half.

Regardless of his many plays prior to 467, a clear distinction
between the *Septem* and the later plays should throw some light on
their special characteristics. If the *Septem* seems in essentials like
these plays, we should be precluded from ascribing any sort of
development or change to Aeschylus' dramaturgy, for the *Persae* in
itself can tell us little. If there is a marked difference, this may be
of considerable significance.

The danger is that of circular reasoning. We cannot reconstruct
the *Prometheia* or *Suppliants* on the basis of the *Oresteia* and then
assume that they confirm the evidence of the *Oresteia*, so that we

1. Albin Lesky, *Die Tragische Dichtung der Hellenen*[3] (Göttingen, 1972) 98
and n. 39.

can in some sense know the true nature of Aeschylus' later drama-turgy. The short span of four years between the *Septem* and the *Suppliants* and the absence of the last two plays of the *Suppliants* trilogy hardly warrant us in drawing conclusions from supposed differences between them. The *Prometheia* is not securely dated and is only one play and not the last or resolving play of its trilogy; it is a rather uncertain piece of evidence. The best procedure is to compare the *Septem* and the *Oresteia* and see how our conclusions from this may serve to explain or not the other members of the late group, for whose existence as a chronological group there is evidence for two trilogies and quite plausible evidence for another (the *Prometheia*).

The *Septem* has in recent years been given an interpretation different from the traditional view. The new interpretation may be said to have originated from an article by Friedrich Solmsen in 1937 and owes much to the work of Harold Patzer and Erwin Wolff.[2] According to this, there is a total change in the attitude of Eteocles when he discovers that he must face his brother Polyneices in battle at the seventh gate of the city. He sees that the curse (*ara*) of his father, Oedipus, is to be worked on him as well as upon his impious brother, that the Olympian and city gods have now aban-doned him, and that he must accept his fate. He goes suddenly berserk, refuses to "flatter" the gods, and accepts his death in an almost cynical spirit. Apollo and the household Erinys (or Ara) have, he sees, cooperated to doom and damn him. Against this, the traditional view, admirably defended by G. M. Kirkwood in a recent article,[3] asserts the constancy and heroism of Eteocles' character throughout the play and sees no particular mystery in the sudden resurgence of the curse of the Erinys in its latter part. Eteocles had from the start heroically accepted his sacrificial death.

It is not necessary for our purposes here to resolve this disputed issue. I am not now convinced of the correctness of my former interpretation along the general line of Patzer and Wolff, especially my acceptance of Wolff's thesis that Eteocles had already deter-mined the seven gatesmen before he could learn the names of their opponents or opposite numbers from the messenger.[4] I feel con-

---

2. Solmsen, "The Erinys in Aeschylus' *Septem*," *Transactions of the American Philological Association* 68 (1937) 197–211; Patzer, "Die dramatische Hand-lung der *Sieben gegen Theben*," *Harvard Studies in Classical Philology* 63 (1958) 97–119; Wolff, "Die Entscheidung des Eteocles in dem *Sieben gegen Theben*," *Harvard Studies in Classical Philology* 63 (1958) 89–95.

3. "Eteocles Oiakostrophos," *The Phoenix* 23 (1969) 9–25.

4. Brooks Otis, "The Unity of the *Seven against Thebes*," *Greek, Roman and Byzantine Studies* 3 (1960) 153–74.

fident that Aeschylus intended the naming of Polyneices as the final opposing gatesman, after Eteocles had appointed all his own leading fighters to the first six gates, to come as a shock—a climax to the tension built up by the messenger's speech and Eteocles' response to it—and that Eteocles then, for the first time, perceived that he was doomed by the paternal Ara. He was no longer a champion of the city and Olympian gods and under their benevolent protection. Instead he had to accept personal combat with his brother and his own ensuing death; the Ara or Erinys and Apollo were not at odds, but at one. His own patriotism and piety counted for no more than the obvious impiety of his brother Polyneices.

What is beyond dispute is the cooperation of the Erinyes with Apollo, that the Olympians had backed Eteocles as the city's defender and chief hero and, at the same time, acquiesced in his personal fate: he had saved the city by sacrificing his own life, and they had cooperated in this double result. The words of the herald here seem quite unambiguous:

> τὰς δ' ἑβδόμας ὁ σεμνὸς ἑβδομαγέτας
> ἄναξ Ἀπόλλων εἵλετ', Οἰδίπου γένει
> κραίνων παλαιὰς Λαΐου δυσβουλίας.   (800–802)

Apollo had carried out in person his punishment of the Labdacids for the disobedience of Laius to his oracular command. The grandchildren—Polyneices and Eteocles—were made to pay for their grandfather's sin. The paternal curse (Oedipus') was fulfilled (πατρὸς . . . ἀραὶ τελεσφόροι, 655, as Eteocles declared). The trilogy ends with the salvation of Thebes, and happily. It is also the tragedy of the house of Laius. The *polis* does not, as in the *Eumenides*, cooperate with the gods in freeing a hero from his family Erinys and guilt. The problem of the *Oresteia*—the breaking of the demonic chain of crimes—is not solved or is "solved" only by a tragic destruction of the family concerned. There is no indication that Eteocles deserved his fate. Though we lack the *Oedipus* and the full story of his curse on his sons, the references to it in the *Septem* imply the innocence of Eteocles and guilt of Polyneices. It may be that Eteocles, unlike the saintly Amphiaraus, was not willing to flatter (σαίνειν, 704) his fate by belatedly beseeching the gods for a succour they would not give (θεῶν διδόντων οὐκ ἂν ἐκφύγοις κακά, 719). It may even be that his acceptance of death was truly heroic and anticipated by him throughout the play (though this still seems to me to contravene the obvious sense of the text), but in any event the "actions" of Apollo and the Olympians, their ambiguous cooperation with the Ara of his crazed father (Οἰδιπόδα βλαψίφρονος, 725), seem very far removed from their concern for justice in the *Oresteia*.

We can say that Aeschylus was dealing in the two trilogies with two different legends and that he could not change so definite a tradition as that of the mutual destruction of the two Theban brothers. It is difficult to see how Aeschylus could have altered the myth in any drastic way and certainly not so as to save Eteocles. It is also difficult to believe that the Aeschylus of the *Oresteia* would have handled the Theban story in the same way or—what is probably closer to the fact—would have handled it at all. There is piety in the *Septem*. Amphiaraus, the saint of the play, accepts his own doom in full reverence for the gods. This is why he seems so redoubtable to the herald: δεινὸς ὃς θεοὺς σέβει, 596. Aeschylus in the *Septem* accepts tragedy with almost "Sophoclean" simplicity. The problematic character of the Ara or Erinys, its relation to the Olympians, the justice of visiting the sins of the fathers on their children, of involving the good in the fate of the guilty (e.g., Amphiaraus)—these key questions are not raised and certainly not answered.

Nor can we escape the feeling that the nonproblematic character of the play is related to its relatively archaic technique. The long scene of the messenger's description of the hostile gatesmen and Eteocles' counter-description of their Theban opponents is extremely effective, especially in its gradual building up of tension: as each gate is successively manned, the determination of Eteocles' own position and fate comes closer and closer, the contrast of opponents more and more relevant to himself. It is hardly dramatic in the Oresteian sense. There is no dramatic fusion of past and present, no true confrontation beyond the repeated one of the "bad" besiegers and the "good" defenders: Amphiaraus, the one exception to the recurrent antitheses, is not an integral part of the drama. We have the impression of an unrolling panorama explained by Eteocles' comments. The difference between Eteocles' obvious patriotism and his tragic fate is moving. The crime of Laius is avenged on the guilty and the innocent, and the moment of Eteocles' innocence or heroism shines out from the dark frame of his ancestral guilt. For this reason there is no essential change; from the time of Laius' disobedience or neglect of Apollo's oracles, the rest of the trilogy is determined. If we accept Patzer's interpretation and regard Eteocles as, for this brief spell, unaware of his approaching doom, then the coming of the doom itself would seem to have a greater dramatic impact. The tragedy is a single predetermined event—Eteocles' death and fulfillment of the curse or punishment for Laius' affront to Apollo—magnified by its gorgeous, martial setting and partially offset by the salvation of the *polis* of Thebes. There is no radical transformation of preexisting circumstances such as the murder of Agamemnon represented. The *Septem* was the last and not the first play of the trilogy.

If we consider the structure of the play, this becomes clearer. Scholars have long debated the genuineness of the final lines of the manuscript text (1005–78), in which the herald announces the city rulers' decision to bury Eteocles but not Polyneices, Antigone declares her intention to disobey their ruling, and the chorus divides into those who support her and those who do not. I shall not try to debate this famous *Streitfrage* here. To suppose that Aeschylus would have introduced a new conflict at the very end of a trilogy seems to me to contravene the essential logic of this or any other trilogy. Thebes has been saved and the crime of Laius expiated by his unfortunate grandchildren. This is the double outcome that Aeschylus intended, as the mixed character of the final chorus or exodos (up to 1004)—their brief joy at Thebes' salvation and their long lament (*threnos*) on Eteocles—would unambiguously indicate.

This question is not germane to my argument. The *Septem* is structured, as Solmsen pointed out, so that the Ara of Oedipus and the aboriginal error of Laius do not emerge, or at least do not have any dramatic impact, until line 653, or more than halfway through the play, when Eteocles sees that he is doomed, that the curse is about to be realized. This return of the dominant motif of the trilogy—whose first two plays deal with Laius and Oedipus respectively—has for good dramatic reasons been temporarily played down in order to develop the heroic character of Eteocles. No effective distinction is made between the brothers Eteocles and Polyneices, or between the Olympians and the Ara of Oedipus, which makes the tragic finale so impressive. Everything has been built up to the moment when the patriotic Eteocles must take his battle position and fight for his city—the moment of his doom!

If we turn to the *Oresteia*, the relation of the structural differences to the ethical-theological differences of the two trilogies will become clear. The *Oresteia* alternates between an emphasis on Zeus and the Olympians and on the family Erinys or Erinyes. Up to the Cassandra kommos of the *Agamemnon* the problem has been Agamemnon's guilt as seen in the context of the Trojan War and the Olympians (Zeus Xenios as motivator of the war, Artemis as motivator of the sacrifice of Iphigenia, the Greek affront to the Olympians by their temple-desecrations at Troy); Clytemnestra's designs are revealed only indirectly, by hints and by a telltale silence. With Cassandra the *daimones* or Erinyes of the house are given a dominating role. Clytemnestra emerges as the evil genius of the trilogy (comparable to Polyneices in the *Septem*). In the *Choephoroe* the initial and rather unemphatic mention of Apollo as the chief motivator of Orestes' matricide is superseded by the different emphasis of the kommos, in which Orestes is seen as the agent of his father's restless spirit and the family Erinyes. His motive is personal vengeance for the horrors of his father's infamous death and burial. He seems for a moment to crave the matricide. At the time of the murder, when the desire shrinks to nothing and Orestes seems on the point of rejecting the snake-role he had voluntarily assumed, the Apolline theme reemerges with Pylades' dramatic breaking of his long silence. At the end the appearance of the Furies seems to disrupt this theme in an ambiguous and fearful conclusion in which once more the demons of the house assert their predominance. This is the indispensable condition of the confrontation of the two divine elements in the *Eumenides*: the trial and the long final kommos bring them to the point of crisis and reconciliation.

The Labdacid trilogy lacks a final resolving and reconciling statement—the equivalent of the *Eumenides*—and also an equivalent precondition, any effective separation of responsibilities and guilts in either the divine or the human sectors. That Agamemnon is less guilty than Clytemnestra and that Orestes is justified, that the Olympians must show their hand against the powers that continue to treat him as guilty, are what makes the *Oresteia* unlike the trilogy of the *Septem*, in which both Eteocles and Polyneices, both Apollo and the Ara, are involved in one indiscriminate guilt and retribution. To say that this difference is in the original myths is to ignore both the choice of myth and the drastic renovation of the myth in the *Oresteia*. Not only is the *Eumenides* an original addition to the story of the house of Atreus (a Hesiodic renewal of the old Stesichorean, Pindaric, and Cyclic motifs), but it is one that requires a complete reformulation of the whole legend, the raising of Agamemnon's murder to a cosmic event. The *Oresteia* is different in *kind* from the Labdacid trilogy, in which the old legend, in its basic plot at least, is not reformulated.

The differentiation of Olympians and Erinys, or Ara, in the *Septem* is embryonic and inconclusive. What happens after line 653 (when the Erinys reemerges) is a logical conclusion to the trilogy, in which there is no effective difference of purpose between the two sets of divine persons. The *Choephoroe* and *Eumenides* employ the same sort of differentiation (or shift of emphasis between Olympians and Erinyes) but use it to effect a polarization of the gods that opens the passage from tragedy to harmony, and to the favorable resolution that the Labdacid trilogy utterly and conspicuously lacks. The problem of the *Septem* to which Solmsen called attention and with which both the new (Patzer, Wolff) and the traditional interpretations have wrestled, was the starting point of the solution of the *Oresteia*. There is no solution in the *Septem*.

The question is whether the *Oresteia* is an isolated exception to what the *Septem* represents, i.e., a powerful but essentially faithful representation of the established myth, or is rather the product of a new phase of Aeschylus' dramaturgy, a new concern with theodicy and ethics. Was Aeschylus deliberately choosing myths that could express his new ideas and enable him to conclude a trilogy with an original addition to his material?

The *Eumenides* has often been looked at as anthropological history, the mythically disguised clash of patriarchal and matriarchal societies.[5] It is hard to see how Aeschylus could have thought in these terms. Matriarchal societies had long been extinct even if they had once existed, a dubious hypothesis in itself. Aeschylus wanted to differentiate the primitive and obscure powers of vengeance from the ethical and rational Olympians and provide a solid theological basis for the justice of the *polis*. The contrast of the roles of father and mother, wife and husband, blood kinship and marriage, was of dramatic importance—given Aeschylus' wish to reconcile two competing rights without an obtrusive overriding of one by the other—but it was a dramatic means to a theological and ethical end which was not the assertion of father-right or husband-right but of divine and human justice.

Where Aeschylus found his material for the arguments of the Furies and Apollo was in contemporary fifth-century physiological theory. Diogenes of Apollonia and Hippon of Metapontum originated or defended the theory advanced by Apollo in the trial, and Alcmaeon of Croton, Parmenides, and Empedocles opposed it. Aeschylus probably found this theory in Sicily (where he resided from 458 on, and which he had visited several times before), since no other Athenian author (save Euripides in the *Orestes* 552–54, where the reference is clearly to Aeschylus) mentions it. Since the *Eumenides* is, in its essential conception and relation to the traditional Atreus myth, an innovation, it provided opportunity for the insertion of such material. Aeschylus had to find arguments for Apollo and a principle of discrimination for his Furies that would keep the trial on the "morally neutral" key that was essential for the eventual reconciliation of the Furies and the Olympians. The *Eumenides* was a novelty demanded by his new "Hesiodic" conception of divine-human relations, his desire to solve the great ethical

5. See George Thompson, *Aeschylus and Athens* (Cambridge, 1940) 278–79.

and theological problems presented to the *polis* and to the individual conscience by the mysterious workings of crime, guilt, and retribution.

Can we find anything of the same sort in the Danaid (*Suppliants*) trilogy and the *Prometheia*? The last (and crucial) two plays in each of these two trilogies are lost and information about them is scant. The relation of the two trilogies has a bearing on our interpretation of each. The *Prometheus Desmotes*, our surviving Prometheian play, constitutes a unique problem in itself. In style and to some extent in content it seems so different, so un-Aeschylean that a few highly reputable scholars have even denied its Aeschylean authorship.[6] This is a desperate remedy for the difficulties involved, and overlooks the indubitably Aeschylean qualities of the play. It points to peculiarities that we ought to take into account. One is the presence of an essentially primitive or preethical Zeus and of a theological aspect to the play and trilogy—a trilogy taking gods, not men, as the primary theme. If men were introduced, as they probably were, in what seems to have been the final play, the *Prometheus Pyrphoros*, they were introduced in a different way from that of the *Oresteia*. The movement in the *Prometheia* is from gods to men and not men to gods, and the change (if change there is) is demanded by a divine, not a human event.

There is a strong assumption that the *Prometheus* is late, though there is not, I think, anything sufficiently definite to date it after the *Oresteia* as some would do.[7] We must account for its peculiar style—which even the ordinary reader notices in its syntactical simplicity and diction, the relative ease with which it can be read— and this seems to demand the assumption of a new approach or phase of development in Aeschylus, an approach that must also be a late approach unless we are to explain away a whole mass of stylistic and other evidence.[8] One, but only one, of the reasons for positing its lateness is its reference to the *Suppliants*. Not only do both plays give prominence to Io, her wanderings, and her involvement with Zeus and Hera, but the *Prometheus* gives us a summary of the material dealt with by the *Suppliants* trilogy.[9] In 853–69 we

6. W. Schmid, *Untersuchungen zum Gefesselten Prometheus*, Tübingen Beiträge 9 (Tübingen, 1929); Mark Griffith, *The Authenticity of "Prometheus Bound"* (Cambridge, 1977).

7. George Thompson, *Aeschylus: "Prometheus Bound"* (Cambridge, 1932) 32.

8. C. J. Herington, *The Author of "Prometheus Bound"* (Austin and London, 1970).

9. R. D. Murray, *The Motif of Io in Aeschylus' "Supplices"* (Princeton, 1958).

are told that of the fifth generation sprung from Io's son Epaphus, the fifty daughters of Danaus will come to Argos, fleeing from a marriage with their cousins, the sons of Aegyptus. They are likened to doves pursued by kites. The marriage is forbidden and banned by the "god" (ἥξουσι θηρεύοντες οὐ θηρασίμους / γάμους, φθόνον δὲ σωμάτων ἕξει θεός, 858–59). The pursuing Egyptians will be buried in Argos after being boldly murdered by the women in the night: each woman (with one exception) will kill her "husband" with the sword. The exception (Hypermnestra, though the name is not given in the *Prometheus*) will be moved by love (ἵμερος, 865) not to kill her husband, or will soften her determination (ἀπαμβλυνθήσεται, 866) to do so. She will choose to be called cowardly (ἄναλκις, 868) rather than murderess (μιαιφόνος, 868). She will bear children who will constitute the royal line of Argos until one of her descendants (Heracles) will by his bow deliver Prometheus from his woes.

We have here a reference to the Danaid trilogy. Aeschylus might have deliberately altered the plot of the trilogy (from that given in the *Prometheus*) or—more probably—altered (in the *Prometheus*) the plot of the earlier *Suppliants*. The summary in the *Prometheus* is so circumstantial, and the role of Io in both plays so prominent, that it is difficult to escape the feeling that there is a direct reference in the *Prometheus* back to the *Suppliants* trilogy. (This argument would, I think, hold even more strongly if Aeschylus were in fact *not* the author of the *Prometheus*, for in that case the unknown author must have known something of the *Suppliants* trilogy.) Aeschylus is saying that Prometheus will finally be released from the horrors of the vulture and inferentially from all his bonds through the mediation of a famous descendant of Zeus and Io, a descendant who represents the rehabilitation or vindication of both Io and Prometheus himself. The drama of the *Suppliants* trilogy fulfills an ancient prophecy and shows how the forced "marriage" of Io (the victim of the old, primitive Zeus, the woman forced against her will into sexual intercourse and cruelly persecuted for it by the jealous Hera) will be recompensed in the fifth or sixth generation by a new marriage of desire or voluntary consent and that this will produce a new generation by whom the old wrongs of Prometheus will be remedied. So Themis herself has told Prometheus. The terrible deed of Hypermnestra's Danaid sisters is described so as to indicate its immorality and horror. In refusing to be a murderess (μιαιφόνος, 868), Hypermnestra inaugurates a new kind of marriage that is represented as the final vindication of Io.

Seen in this light—a light that comes from Aeschylus himself or at least from an author who in all probability knew Aeschylus'

Suppliants trilogy—that trilogy can be made intelligible even if it cannot be reconstructed. We know almost nothing of the second play, the *Egyptians*, and possess but two fragments of what is almost certainly the third play, the *Danaids*.[10] If we follow the clue of the *Prometheus* and assume that the *Egyptians* must have dealt with the terrible marriage or with the negotiations leading to it and that the *Danaids* contained some account of the true marriage and rehabilitation of Hypermnestra, we can see how the *Suppliants*, as supplemented by one significant fragment from the *Danaids* and the interpretative framework of the *Prometheus*, can throw light on the meaning of the whole trilogy.

The *Suppliants* opens without a prologue. The chorus of Danaids enters chanting a march-prelude of anapaests and calling on Zeus Aphiktor, Zeus the protector of suppliants. The immediate reason for the subject of the parodos is their need to prove to the people of Argos that they are Argives by their descent from Io. This is a pretext for introducing the Io motif that is basic to the play. The long parodos (135 lines) emphasizes the ambivalence of their relation to both Io and Zeus. Zeus is the cruel male pursuer of Io as Hera is her implacable enemy; the divine wrath that once pursued Io now pursues them:

> ἆ Ζήν, Ἰοῦς· ἰὼ μῆνις
> μάστειρ' ἐκ θεῶν·   (162–63)

Zeus is the god of suppliants, the god of justice who should defend them against the *hybris* of their Egyptian cousins (77–87). In language similar to the hymn to Zeus in the *Agamemnon*, the Danaids recognize both the obscurity and the effortless power of Zeus' justice (91–92). Zeus will be subjected to unjust words (οὐ δικαίοις . . . λόγοις, 168–69) if he turns away from the offspring of the cow (Io), which is his own offspring. Zeus is at once the principal of a morally dubious episode in the past (though the blame is more Hera's than his) and the god of justice. His wooing of Io is analogous to the Egyptians' wooing of the Danaids, and his moral eminence is invoked against the Egyptians' hybristic attempt to do erotic violence to them.

There has been much debate as to why the Danaids are so opposed to marriage with their cousins. There is no indication that the proposed marriage is formally illegal or incestuous, or that it is even abnormal or unusual. What is clear is that the Egyptians show *hybris*, that they want to attain their end by force and violence, against the will of the girls. There is no mutuality of love

10. A. F. Garvie, *Aeschylus' "Supplices": Play and Trilogy* (Cambridge, 1969).

or desire. The girls are not controlled by their father Danaus or
forced to defer to his will rather than their own. They show an
almost Amazonian strength and reveal emotions that are their
own. They dominate the play, causing scholars, before the publication of the papyrus, to assume its early date; it represented a
period when tragedy was mostly chorus. The contrary is nearer
the truth: the chorus is prominent because the Danaids are active
and full of initiative. What are we to think of their initiative?

They do seem to represent justice vis à vis the Egyptians, who
by both their violent attempt to force the marriage and their reckless indifference to the rights of the suppliants, show *hybris* in the
clearest way. The parodos, which sets the tone of the whole play,
is ambivalent. Zeus and the gods are ambivalent; the case of Io is
altogether too like the suppliants' own to make Zeus' *dike* reliable.
Nor is their own case without ambivalence. While they are right
in fleeing a forced marriage, they are regarded as wrong in extrapo-
lating their fear of *this* marriage into aversion to *any* marriage. The
therapinae, or attendants, at the end of the play, make this very
clear. As Kurt von Fritz has pointed out, their warning to the
Danaids is a foreshadowing of the turn of events in the next play of
the trilogy.[11] The *hybris* of the Egyptians, like that of Agamemnon,
yields to the *hybris* of their punishers. The Danaids are one link in
a chain of vengeance, and the *hybris* of their vengeance will overtop
the original *hybris* that caused it.

First the girls demand that Pelasgos, the Argive king, accept
them as suppliants in spite of the danger of war that must follow
his consent. He complies when they threaten to profane the gods
by hanging themselves from their images. Their harsh treatment
by the Egyptian herald and his attendants justifies their rescue by
Pelasgos and reception into the city. The girls' insistent objection
to the marriage becomes a terrible threat to the people of Argos
and Pelasgos, who had no quarrel with the Egyptians. Any *hybris*
on the girls' part—any carrying of their objection to marriage
beyond reasonable grounds—reacts upon their noble protectors.
Pelasgos is caught in his own dilemma: he cannot assess the marriage on its own merits, because he is forced by the girls' threat to
avoid the danger of sacrilege. Zeus' role as Aphiktor, as protector
of the suppliants, overlaps his role as ancestor and bedfellow of Io.
What stands out in the play is the *hybris* of the Egyptians, piety of
the Argives, and ambiguous motivation of the Danaids.

11. "Die Danaiden Trilogie des Aeschylus," *Philologus* 91 (1936) 121–
36, 249–69; reprinted in his *Antike und Moderne Tragödie* (Berlin, 1962)
160–92.

The Egyptians in one way or another seem to have compelled their consent to the marriage. Pelasgos may have been killed in battle with them and Danaus, the girls' father, then assumed the kingship of Argos. Their marriage to the Egyptians was agreed to, though with the secret understanding between Danaus and the girls that each should kill her husband on the wedding night. We do not know how this was presented in the *Egyptians* or (possibly) in the following *Danaids*. A brief fragment indicates that someone (presumably Danaus) gave orders to serenade the newlyweds on the morning after the wedding night. It may belong at the beginning of the last play, the *Danaids*, but this is far from certain: it might belong to the previous play or even at the end of the *Danaids* (referring then to the recent marriage of the Danaids).

The last play, the *Danaids*, dealt with the consequences of the fatal wedding night. Was it the subsequent purification and re-marriage of the Danaids? Was it the exoneration of Hypermnestra? Was it both? The Danaids were not condemned to death (the legend about their post-mortem punishment in Hades is later) but were purified of blood-guilt and freed to marry other men, pos-sibly, as Pindar has indicated (*Pythian* 9.111–16), by being given as prizes to the victors of races or games in an *agon*, or athletic event. Von Fritz has argued at some length that this was the sub-ject of the *Danaids* and that there was not enough room in such a closely-knit trilogy for the story of Hypermnestra or the "trial" that some ancient authors describe as the means of her acquittal from the charge of "disobeying" her father Danaus.

Aphrodite appeared in this play and proclaimed the high and universal validity of love: *eros* as the cause of all the unions or har-monies of nature and as the supreme principle of creation. This is the clue to the whole matter if we are justified in interpreting it in the light of the *Prometheus* passage. It has been argued that Aphro-dite's remarks would not fit a scene condemning the Danaids. Von Fritz thinks that they suit the new marriage *after* the purification.[12] Could Aphrodite have addressed her splendid panegyric of true *eros* only to the murderous Danaids? Could the Danaids have been exonerated? The *Prometheus'* emphasis on Hypermnestra, as well as her subsequent place in legend, makes it difficult to believe that she could have been left out.

The decisive reason for believing that Hypermnestra played a prominent role in the play is that her husband Lynceus was the sole surviving Aegyptiad and that it was from his marriage to Hypermnestra that the subsequent line of Argos (including

12. "Danaiden Trilogie," 249–61; reprint 173–84.

Heracles) descended. The wrong of the Aegyptiads had been countered by the wrong of the Danaids, an impious forced marriage by an impious murder plot. Aeschylus could hardly have left the wrongdoers in assured possession, nor could he have eliminated the entire house of Aegyptus in the face of all tradition and in spite of his own concern to reach some solution to the problem of forced versus voluntary marriage, as well as a solution to the problem of Zeus' *dike*, the problem that had been so prominently raised in the parodos of the *Suppliants*. The Danaids are more to blame than the Aegyptiads, and that is the reason (in terms of a drama concerned with love and justice) why at least one Aegyptiad must survive and figure prominently in the conclusion.

Aphrodite appeared on the Argive scene to do justice to all, punishing the Danaids by forcing them to undergo a new marriage and to become willy-nilly the prizes of victors on the racecourse, and rewarding Hypermnestra by confirming her and her husband's marriage and eventual authority (kingship) in Argos. The occasion called for an explanation of true *eros* and of its universal significance. *Eros* was not a destructive passion, a violent disruption of female virtue and human justice, but the creative originator of all new things. The Danaids and the Egyptians did not understand this, with the conspicuous and crucial exceptions of Lynceus and Hypermnestra. Whether this scene took the form of a trial or not, and what role Danaus may have played in the matter, are questions that cannot be answered. The trilogy ends with an exaltation and justification of love and marriage (ἔρως δὲ γαῖαν λαμβάνει γάμου τυχεῖν),[13] and this is represented as divine and approved by Zeus. Both the one-sided violence of the Egyptians and the fanatical chastity of the Danaids are condemned, as is the positive injustice to which both led. Lynceus and Hypermnestra are the good lovers who survive and triumph. The offspring of Zeus and Io have realized the meaning of true marriage and true *dike*. While we do not get a clear differentiation of orders of gods, as in the *Oresteia*, we get a differentiation of good and bad loves and a divine declaration to that effect. Instead of the tragic ending of the *Septem* we find the right and power of true, united love: the ambiguities of the parodos are cleared up.

The *Prometheia* is the most "Hesiodic" of all Aeschylus' dramas. It is concerned from the start with the different generations of the gods and does not bring the gods in at the end as do the *Oresteia* and the Danaid trilogy. It is the resolution of the *Prometheia* that

13. Aeschylus fragment 125.21 in Hans Joachim Mette, *Die Fragmente der Tragödien des Aischylos* (Berlin, 1959) 44.

remains obscure. This is not true of the *Suppliants* trilogy, for which we have the crucial fragment from Aphrodite's speech and the summary from the *Prometheus*. These tell us that the trilogy dealt with an event, the murder of the Aegyptiads, which was at once the culmination of an old conflict, a conflict of sexes, and the beginning of a new harmony—the recognition and acceptance by those concerned of the beneficent power of *eros*. Just as in the *Agamemnon* the *dike* of Zeus is involved and cannot be left ambiguous, the perplexities of the Io-Zeus relationship are exemplified in their descendants, who carry out a process that Io and Zeus had begun. To say that Zeus and the Ionides are reconciled by Aphrodite would perhaps be going beyond the evidence at our disposal, but both Danaids and Aegyptiads have misconceived the present purposes of Zeus and Aphrodite, and the roots of this misconception lie deep in the cosmic past. Not only Aphrodite but Zeus himself (his *dike*) inaugurates a new era. The murder of the Aegyptiads brings the issue or problem of *eros* and *dike* to a head, and leads to a resolution in which the *polis* of Argos is included.

There is no tragic separation of the fate of a *polis* from that of its reigning house, such as we see in the *Septem*, no ambiguous cooperation of great gods and *daimones* in the extinction of a family. The *Suppliants* trilogy is no tragedy in this sense; as in the *Agamemnon*, the murder is the vehicle of a change, and what we know of the last play, the *Danaids*, reveals that change in effect. The lack of the last two plays prevents us from observing the technique, but the *Suppliants* by itself offers some significant indications. The violent opposition of the two sides—Danaids and Aegyptiads—and the *aporia* or helplessness (ἀμηχανίη, cf. 379) of the unfortunate middleman, Pelasgos, are different from the conflict we find in the *Septem*. The latter could have only one outcome—both men and gods had so determined—but the other is ambiguous and open. Nor is this simply because the *Septem* concludes and the *Suppliants* opens a trilogy. In the Labdacid trilogy, everything since the murder of Laius has been determined by the myth itself, but fundamentally by the underlying conception of the divine will. We know how the gods will act. But the divine will in the *Suppliants*, like that in the *Agamemnon*, (this is especially evident in the two parodoi), is ambiguous. Both Aegyptiads and Danaids, both Agamemnon and Clytemnestra, are wrong; their wrong is involved in a right which cannot be eliminated but which perforce requires a new sort of divine intervention. Though many may die in the process, the process is going beyond tragedy, and the poet himself is going beyond the fixed myths and legends that did not provide him with sufficient openness or fluidity for his nontragic resolution. We could not have deduced the transformation of the Furies into Eumenides or the intervention of Aphrodite in the *Danaids*, from information available outside the plays. We have to reckon with the poet as well as the myth.

The *Prometheia* presents us with more of a problem. There is, in the *Prometheus Desmotes*, no parodos that declares the validity of Zeus' *dike* and the ambiguity in which it is hidden. The chorus of Oceanids is a thorough partisan of Prometheus—as, in his muddled and prudential way, is Oceanus himself. Io, like Prometheus, is a victim of Zeus and a victim of Hera. Zeus himself is a highly truculent figure, relying only on Force and Might (Kratos and Bia); he hates mankind. His henchmen, Hephaistos and Hermes, are either reluctant or cruel; they show his character in a bad light. This "Hesiodic" Zeus is seen in a moral perspective which emphasizes the disjunction of his justice from his power. Prometheus comes from an older generation—he is the son of Gaia-Themis—and depends on his superior knowledge of the curse of Kronos to square his account with Zeus. So far, every ruling god has been overthrown by his son. There is no reason to expect that Zeus will be an exception, especially if he pursues the violent course upon which he has already embarked. By contrast, Prometheus is a sympathetic figure. When Zeus wanted to destroy weak, defenseless mankind, Prometheus gave it fire and all the arts of civilization. His suffering is the consequence of his philanthropy.

Such a Zeus cannot be more than a transitory figure, a phase in the evolution of a god. Aeschylus could not possibly have preserved so unfavorable an image of the supreme god to the end of his trilogy. The difference from the Zeus of the *Agamemnon* and *Suppliants* paradoi would have been shocking. We have an alternative: either the Zeus of the *Prometheus* evolves into a god of justice, benevolently interested in mankind, or Aeschylus is not the author of the play and trilogy. Such an alternative is an impossible dilemma. Assuming that we accept the authorship of Aeschylus—and not to do so is to take a *very* great liberty with the ancient tradition—are we justified in positing the "consistency" of his theology or in imposing the evidence of the *Suppliants* and *Oresteia* on the *Prometheia* despite the fact that the *Prometheus* seems to contradict it? Is this not a *petitio principii* of the grossest kind? There is some evidence for asserting the congruence or dramatic and theological agreement of the *Suppliants* trilogy and *Oresteia*. We do not have to devise a question-begging completion of the *Suppliants* trilogy out of knowledge derived from the *Oresteia*. This is not true of the *Prometheia*. We cannot complete the *Prometheia* from the *Oresteia* and *Suppliants* trilogy and then use our conclusion as evidence for a common Aeschylean theology or "late phase" of Aeschylean dramaturgy.[14]

What we can do is develop, from the extant *Prometheus Desmotes* itself, the consequences of Aeschylean authorship. The problem revolves around the last play, which is presumably (though not certainly) the *Prometheus Pyrphoros*. The title suggests that it dealt with the initial theft of fire for which Prometheus was punished in the extant play. The *Desmotes* seems to mark a beginning, and the copious allusions in it to the fire-theft, especially as set in the elaborate context of Prometheus' civilizing activities, seem to be more than references to a previous drama. It would be hard to imagine a dramatic presentation of the actual fire-theft and fire-bringing. This is why Rudolf Westphal's suggestion that the *Pyrphoros* refers to a later "thank-festival" at which was established the Athenian cult of Prometheus as the πυρφόρος θεός, mentioned in Sophocles' *Oedipus Coloneus* (55–56), seems so plausible.[15] It is possible to connect this festival with two Aeschylean lines quoted by the Homeric scholiast Porphyry (though unfortunately without mention of a specific play) and with some papyrus fragments that seem to refer to either the *Prometheus Pyrphoros* or *Prometheus Pyrkaeus* (a play from a quite different trilogy).[16] We are told in several ancient sources (especially Athenaeus)[17] that Prometheus, on release from his Caucasian bondage, was forgiven by Zeus and "crowned" by the mortals who had benefited from his gift of fire. Unfortunately all this evidence is anything but solid. Westphal's hypothesis is the most plausible solution of what and where the *Pyrphoros* was, i.e., that it was not the first but the last play of the trilogy and represented the complete rehabilitation of Prometheus as a philanthropic god, fully forgiven and even honored by Zeus himself. This requires a rather drastic change of Zeus' character from that presented in the *Desmotes*.

Prometheus was released from bondage (we have evidence from the *Desmotes* itself and numerous references in fragments of the second play, the *Prometheus Luomenos*, as well as its very title), Heracles came and shot the vulture or eagle with his arrow, and Zeus somehow made up the quarrel. This we know. Prometheus probably warned Zeus of his fatal marriage in sufficient time for

---

14. C. J. Herington, "Aeschylus: The Last Phase," *Arion* 4 (1965) 1387–1408.

15. *Prolegomena zu Aischylos' Tragödien* (Leipzig, 1869) Anhang, 206.

16. Aeschylus fragments 343–50, Mette 126–31; *Aeschylus*, ed. Hugh Lloyd-Jones (Cambridge, Mass. and London, 1956) 562–66.

17. Aeschylus fragment 334, Mette 123–24.

the latter to change his plans and bestow Thetis on a mortal (Peleus); the release was a sort of *quid pro quo*, though we have no sure knowledge of how the whole transaction was carried out.

None of this establishes the moral evolution of Zeus. Solmsen has carefully pointed out the "moralization" of Hesiod in the *Desmotes*.[18] The moral problem of Zeus' treatment of either Prometheus or mankind did not obtrude upon the writers of the *Theogony* or the account of Prometheus in our text of that work (its actual authorship is not here important; at any rate this is the "Hesiod" that Aeschylus knew). The Hesiodic view of mankind (especially womankind) is pessimistic: the progressive and optimistic conception of civilization in our *Prometheus* is non-Hesiodic. The picture of Zeus presented in the *Desmotes* is that of a primitive god, uncertain of his power and overassertive. The permanent status of Zeus is still in doubt. All his predecessors (Ouranos, Kronos) have been overthrown by their own children because of their unbearable behavior. Prometheus had gone over to Zeus' side in his battle with the Titans and had provided the cleverness which had gained the victory that force could not secure. Zeus' ingratitude, hatred of mankind, and continued dependence on force are the respects in which his moral inferiority to Prometheus seems clearest.

The "new" gods have not as yet asserted any *dike* among either men or fellow gods. In addition to Zeus, Hermes and Hera are depicted as amoral. The difference of generations is not, as in the *Eumenides*, one in which the older is the more primitive and amoral, but one in which the odds are divided: Zeus is better than the Titans but not better than Prometheus or Gaia or a number of the older divinities (like Oceanus). The *Desmotes* is explicitly moralistic, explicitly critical of the primitive morality, the dependence on force rather than reason and justice, apparent in the actions of Zeus. Prometheus' defiance of Zeus may not be fully justified, but the play gives no warrant for equalizing the blame between Zeus and himself, or denying the moral criticism to which Zeus is subjected.

The only way in which we can reconcile the moral bias of the *Desmotes* with the conception of Zeus in Aeschylus' other plays, especially the *Oresteia* and *Suppliants* trilogy, is to conclude that the reprehensibly amoral Zeus of the *Desmotes* did undergo a change (one leading to a genuine reconciliation with Prometheus and mankind). There is some reason to draw such a conclusion from the evidence we have for the trilogy. A token reconciliation of Zeus and Prometheus, of Zeus and mankind, did take place; there is too

18. *Hesiod and Aeschylus* (Ithaca, 1949) 124–77, esp. 138–57.

much evidence from ancient sources to make this doubtful. It is hard to believe that this *de facto* reconciliation was not moralized in a way analogous to the moralization of Hesiod in the *Desmotes*. Aeschylus could not have subjected Zeus to moral criticism in the *Desmotes* and not also subjected him to a more positive moral appraisal in the later plays, in which the situation of the *Desmotes* was changed. In a dramatic work, this could only mean the emergence of a juster Zeus.

Such a conclusion is more than we can derive solely from the *Desmotes* and the scant evidence for the rest of the trilogy. If we disregard that evidence and the evidence of the other extant plays, then we can only settle for an iconoclastic play that can hardly be attributed to Aeschylus. We should be required to treat the *Prometheus Desmotes* as a single play and deny that it was ever part of a trilogy.[19] Assuming that we do not come to such a conclusion (to do otherwise, would require an unwarranted skepticism toward the available evidence), we can settle one question that has in recent years dogged critical discussion of the *Prometheia*. This is the often-stated objection that an evolutionary concept of the divine is alien to the ancient Greek world.[20] There is no need here to import either the label or the idea of evolution or development: the question is simply whether or not the *Prometheia* is like the *Oresteia* (and also, perhaps, the *Suppliants* trilogy, though its lacunae make comparisons difficult) in its conception of a change or transformation in the character of its divinities, above all in the relations of the older and newer strata of divinities. To such a question the answer suggests itself. If we know that the Erinyes did change their nature, why should we not suppose that the Zeus of the *Prometheia* did not?

It is not only the Erinyes who change in the *Oresteia*. The murder of Agamemnon demanded a new initiative from the Olympians and a new relationship to the old gods of criminal retribution. We are likewise justified in pointing to something new in Aphrodite's appearance in the *Danaids*. The *Prometheia* is more daring than the *Oresteia* or the *Suppliants* trilogy: the theology is directly explained, not subjected to the puzzled thinking of the human characters. It is at bottom a similar piece of "Hesiodic" reconstruction. Man is associated with two generations of gods whose initial relationships have not been settled and who cannot establish a viable system of human or divine justice. In the *Oresteia* and *Suppliants* trilogy the decisive action begins in the human sector—men take the initiative—whereas it is the gods who act and initiate in the *Prometheia*. If we are right about the *Pyrphoros*, then gods (certainly Prometheus) come down to earth, or at least make their presence felt on earth, and enter the *polis* of Athens. The whole quarrel of Zeus and Prometheus has been about mankind, while their reconciliation is an essential condition of man's civilization and very survival. The drama is one of change, one in which a single event takes on cosmic significance and so changes the cosmic balance of power or balance of justice. It is much more impressive when the change is a human event cosmically magnified than when it is a divine event reduced to its human implications. The latter procedure carries with it an unavoidable element of anticlimax. As drama, the *Oresteia* stands out and would stand out if the whole *Prometheia* were still in existence—and I might even add, all the rest of Aeschylus as well.

The object of this discussion has been to consider the applicability of our analysis of the *Oresteia* to the other trilogies of Aeschylus. It is not applicable to the *Septem* or its trilogy but is within limits applicable to the *Prometheus* and *Suppliants*. The drama of the *Septem* is action within a settled cosmos or a predetermined *status quo* which no character—human or divine—subjects to moral demands or an essential reformulation. The necessary conjunction of fate and freedom, divine planning and human action, is accepted and taken for granted. The pious man like Amphiaraus reverently submits to his doom. The hiddenness of the gods' decrees is part of the system: men cannot expect to know much and the gods have no intention of clearing things up. How different is the atmosphere of the three late trilogies! Tragedies and catastrophes still occur but they are not final; they are the precondition of a new heaven and a new earth. "Tragedy" like this requires a new technique, a "swelling" of the moment of action into a panoramic past-present so that we have the feeling of a whole *status quo* in jeopardy and a new *status quo* in the offing.

We are, by the accidents of preservation, thrown back on the *Oresteia*, our sole extant trilogy. We can with the exercise of due caution see similarities and differences between it and its two more or less contemporary trilogies. The *Suppliants* resembles the early sections of the *Agamemnon* in its lyrical emphasis and its gradual buildup of the decisive event—the brutal killing. The long negotiations with Pelasgos and the Argives anticipate the coming of the Aegyptiads (this is why the Danaids are so concerned with a speedy asylum), and the dramatic *attentat* of the herald brings the eventual conflict still nearer. The final countering of the Danaids or "man-shunning" (φυξανορία, 9) by the *Therapinae*, their mention of Cypris-Aphrodite as the power of the play, foreshadows the next stage in the manner of the finale of the *Choephoroe*. The *Prometheus* builds up the resentment of the bound giant as he is progressively exposed to enemies, friends, and fellow sufferers (Io) until he incurs that renewed wrath of Zeus against which he has been repeatedly warned. The might of Zeus is exerted against the power of Prometheus' secret weapon, the curse of Kronos, and the tension of the opposition must break. The important thing in all three trilogies is the nature rather than the fact of conflict and tension: this is the essential ambiguity, both ethical and actual, of actions which do not admit of a merely tragical or merely optimistic outcome, but point to a clarification of the issues and a final transcendence of tragedy. The gods can no longer keep their secrets or old obscurities; they go through conflict into harmony.

The *Oresteia* is unique in its peculiar combination of cosmic-theological and historical-legendary elements. The myths of the *Prometheia* and Danaid trilogy are ethereal, exotic, unearthly. The barbaric Egyptians and Danaids are much more and much less than Argives or Greeks; their emotions are as excessive as their deeds, and they subject the Argives to an almost unbearable strain. Zeus and Io are revived in human shape, and the moral ambiguity of *eros* assumes a strange and terrible form. The *Prometheia* is wholly ahistorical. The struggle that lasts thirty thousand years utterly dwarfs a merely human perspective. The *Oresteia* is concerned with a tangible historical event, the Trojan War, and tangible historical figures, Agamemnon, Clytemnestra, and Orestes. The raising of their tragedy to cosmic dimensions is peculiarly impressive, a linking of two worlds, or of history and myth, of Homer and Hesiod. Common to all three trilogies is a new conception of myth. Aeschylus could not invent new myths or legends but he could choose relatively fluid ones, legends with largely indefinite outcomes, so that his return to Hesiod would not be stopped by the limitation of his plots.

This raises the question of his immense production before 467, the date of the *Septem*. To what extent was the *Septem* the last or close to the last of the plays of the "old" manner and subject matter? Can we properly think of it as typical of all the trilogies written before the final phase that we can reasonably date from the *Suppliants* of 463? The connected trilogies of which we have some record of each play are as follows (I omit the extant or partially extant trilogies already discussed); *Argonauts* (*Argo, Lemnians, Hypsipyle*); *Lycurgeia* (*Hedonoi, Bassarai, Neaniskoi*); *Achilleis* (*Myrmidons,*

Nereids, Phrygians or *Ransom of Hector*); *Ajax* (*Hoplon Krisis, Thressians, Salaminians*); *Dionysus* (*Semele, Pentheus, Xantriae*); *Odysseus* (*Psychagogoi, Penelope, Ostrologoi*). Trilogies of which we have information of two (of the three) plays are: *Memnon, Ixion, Sisyphus, Philoctetes, Telephos,* and *Perseus.* Certainly there were more trilogies: the catalogue of Aeschylean plays lists seventy-three titles, some of which may have constituted trilogies whose exact composition is unknown to us.

There is no reason to doubt that there were a number of unconnected trilogies or tetralogies of plays, of which the *Persae* is the extant example. A survey of titles and fragments indicates nothing that would lead us to suppose a "Hesiodic" intent or an anticipation of the later dramaturgy as we have defined it. It is difficult to imagine that the *Achilleis, Argonauts, Ajax, Odysseus, Memnon, Philoctetes,* or *Perseus* trilogies represented any radical reformulation of the well-known myths or of Homer. The same can be said of the two Dionysiac trilogies (concerned with Pentheus and Lycurgus). None of these myths were "fluid," as were those about the Furies, the Danaids, or Prometheus.

This hypothesis is confirmed by the *Persae* of 472. We cannot draw too many conclusions from the relatively "static" quality of this play. That the action is past and is related by a messenger, supplemented by the ghost of Darius and the words of Xerxes at the end, is due to the subject matter and possibly to the example of Phrynichus' *Phoenissae.* This is near-contemporary history, not malleable myth. Aeschylus could hardly have treated the latter in the same static way and he had used myth in some of the trilogies cited above, well before 472. The static format of the *Persae* reveals a conception of the divine-human relationship that is similar to that of the *Septem* and can hardly have been different in the lost *Ajax, Philoctetes,* or *Odysseus* trilogies. The central idea of the play is revealed by the ghostly Darius: Zeus had through oracles prophesied the doom of Xerxes, but Darius had prayed the gods to defer its execution "for a long time" (διὰ μακροῦ χρόνου, 741). But the mad Xerxes (θούριος Ξέρξης, 718, 754) had instead hastened his fate and the gods had gladly cooperated. He had—mortal that he was—disregarded the Immortals and in particular tried to enchain Poseidon (the sea) by his attempt to bridge the Hellespont. A great *daimon,* as Atossa remarked, had taken away his wits (724). Xerxes' defeat is attributed to his own impiety, his evil *daimon,* and the general ill-will of the gods—not to the courage of the Greeks. Such a conception can justly be called primitive; it is very close to Homer. There is no clear-cut demarcation of divine will and human guilt; both are indissolubly conjoined. There is no attempt to distinguish between the Olympians and other gods such as Xerxes' "big *daimon*" (725). The obscurity of the divine will is taken for granted, though room is made for human folly or guilt. It makes things easier for the gods, who are glad to hurry up the doom that is in any event only a matter of time.

We must not suppose that all the other trilogies of Aeschylus were tragedies like the *Septem* or *Persae*. But insofar as he did write tragedy, there is no reason to think that he advanced in either his ethics or his theology beyond the *Septem*. Five years separate it from the *Persae*. Many of his "connected" early trilogies are loosely connected, and some plays in the trilogies are not connected at all. The conception of the *Oresteia* or of the *Suppliants* trilogy and the *Prometheia* was not in all human probability the product of a young man but of one who had already passed through a lifetime of thought and dramatic experience. His ability to write three dramas around one cosmic event, or one human event with cosmic consequences, so that the event itself took on a new dramatic significance, constituting a new sort of tragedy, can most plausibly be explained as the product of his final years. It is a pity that we cannot trace his development. It is some consolation to think that there must have been solid grounds for the selection of the seven plays that we have.

We have so far concentrated on the differences between the plays (especially the *Persae* and *Septem* on the one hand and the three final trilogies on the other). This is not to say that there is no common Aeschylean style or content. The tragic sense of the *Persae* and *Septem*, the way they build up tension, their ethical seriousness, their metaphorical and syntactical structure, the choice of "pomp-bundled" or multiply expressive words, are like those of the *Oresteia* or are at least characteristic of one developing style and thought. The difference is primarily one of dramatic movement and theological understanding, each joined in a quite indissoluble combination. In a word, Aeschylus found the direction he wanted to take, the solution he wished to reach, and this galvanized his final trilogies into a new drama, the drama of cosmic change or of cosmic change in inextricable conjunction with ethical and political change.

Why such a transformation in his outlook? Why the emergence of "cosmic tragedy" after 463 or thereabouts? Why did Hesiod speak to Aeschylus at just this time? In one sense the answer is easy: he belonged to a world that was rethinking the Greek mythological inheritance, and understandably, he became receptive to the ethical and cosmic thought of his time. But Aeschylus was not a philosopher or a cosmologist, but a tragedian. When we say that his Sicilian experience exposed him to Western philosophy or that for some other reason he became "receptive to the ethical and cosmic thought of his time" (we lack the biographical data to speak with certainty), we are saying that Aeschylus did not just insert a few Xenophanes-like dicta in his later dramas, but was moved by new ideas to reconstitute the technique and essential nature of his dramaturgy. This has not as yet been clearly perceived. Why so many scholars have been reluctant to attribute significance to the more or less plausible parallels between Aeschylus' descriptions of Zeus in the parodoi of the *Suppliants* and *Agamemnon* and the theological pronouncements of Xenophanes or Heraclitus, for example, is their inability to square these descriptions with the *dramatic* statements of the plays. To say that Zeus is a morally transcendent omnipotent deity—directing all things by his passionless, effortless will—is not to say something very meaningful unless it is translated into the terms of the dramas themselves. If Zeus is the all-powerful teacher of wisdom by suffering, in what way are the vengeance of Artemis, the bloodthirstiness of the Erinyes, the treatment of Cassandra by Apollo, not to mention Zeus' own cruelty in the *Prometheus Desmotes*, consistent with such an idea?

Our analysis of the *Oresteia*, and to a lesser extent our briefer analyses of the *Suppliants* and *Prometheus* trilogies, has indicated a partial answer. The parodoi of the *Agamemnon* and *Suppliants* state not fact but an unrealized idea. The choruses feel that Zeus ought to be what he is not, or what is hidden in the "womb of time." We cannot divorce the great hymns to Zeus of the *Agamemnon* and *Suppliants* parodoi from the obvious doubt and puzzlement of the choruses in both the same parodoi and in the ensuing stasima and episodes. Even the shocking contrast of the transcendent and holy Zeus of these parodoi with the cruel and vengeful Zeus of the *Prometheus Desmotes* is much reduced, almost eliminated when we set the hymns to Zeus in their total dramatic context. Are the Artemis of the *Agamemnon*, the Apollo of the *Eumenides*, so calm and transcendent? Is the superiority of Zeus to the other Olympians so obvious? Aeschylus had to work with the myths he had, with a far from moral theology. The difference between the justice of his mythological sources and that of his Athenian *polis* or Eleatic philosophy (if so it may for convenience be labeled) was evident. Only by positing some sort of cosmic or theological change could he remove so gross an inconsistency. He turned to Hesiod to give himself a precedent for introducing such change into his mythical material.

But Hesiod was not concerned with the same problems as Aeschylus. He did not write dramas based on heroic or Mycenaean

legend, and his major works—the *Theogony* and *Works and Days*—
are not based on such legends. He was centuries removed in time
and in this sense "primitive" as seen from Aeschylus' mid–fifth-
century perspective. The Aeschylean was not identical with the
Hesiodic *dike*. What mattered for Aeschylus' *drama* was not Hesiod's ethical doctrine but the means by which an ethical change
could be theologically accomplished. It was Hesiod that gave
Aeschylus the means.

What was prior to Hesiod, in Aeschylus' mind, was a concern
with moral reality or with the evident immorality of the myth and
religion available to him. It would seem foolish to disregard the
ethical and theological thought of Aeschylus' time, the fact that a
generation of sixth- and fifth-century thinkers had been struggling
with the ethical difficulties of myth and religion. What is distinctive about the later Aeschylus is not his bare "ideology" but his
incorporation of it in a mythical, dramatic form, and most specifically, his use of Hesiod to inaugurate a partial reformulation of
myth and of its theological premises. He saw that the available
myths were based on a primitive or "Homeric" ethic—how could
he possibly have failed to see that?—but he could not deny the
presence of that ethic. His dramatic form prevented him from
taking even the liberties of choral lyrists like Stesichorus or Pindar.
Some myths provided him with a certain freedom, were to a degree
malleable and open-minded. In them he could find room for a
Hesiodic transformation of the divinities involved, though within
the limits of his poetical and dramatic conventions.

What this meant in practice we have already seen in our analysis
of the *Oresteia*. Here the murder of Agamemnon is represented as
the beginning of a process of polarization—a separation of old and
new deities—so that in the end, there is a learning by suffering, a
transformation of both divine and human justice, an approxima-
tion at least to the transcendent purpose of the Zeus of the parodos.
In the *Prometheia* it is probable that the Zeus who was a true son of
Kronos—like him both violent and unjust—became receptive of
the ethic by which he had been in the *Prometheus Desmotes* both
explicitly and implicitly condemned. In the *Suppliants* trilogy, the
Zeus of the parodos does seem to have guided the way or at least to
have given sanction to Aphrodite's final proclamation of a universal
and beneficent *eros*, a way that was also that of his own divine
experience. About the *Prometheia* and the Danaid trilogy there cannot in the nature of things be anything like certainty. The *Oresteia*
indicates the nature of Aeschulus' thought in one phase of his
dramaturgy. It shows us what a drama of cosmic change can be.

Without his inheritance of myth and dramatic convention (the dramatic use of myth) he could never have written his tragedies at all; without his knowledge and use of Hesiod he could not have given them a contemporary turn; and without his interest in the new ethical and philosophical ideas of his time he would never have resorted to Hesiod at all. To say this is to oversimplify Aeschylus' problem. But it does bring out the significance of his dramatic method, more precisely the significance of his dramatic use of Hesiod. His importance is not due to his ideas as such but to his reconstitution of tragedy, his creation of an art form in which tragedy could achieve a good or optimistic result without ceasing to be itself. He purchased a cosmic good at a price that was still preeminently tragic. This was his distinctive dramatic achievement.